SOCIAL SKILLS

Useful tips to Improve Your Social Intelligence, Social Circle and Win Friends, Build Better Relationships and Achieve Success in Private and at Work

© Copyright 2021

All rights reserved.

This report is towards furnishing precise and reliable data concerning the point and issue secured. It was conceivable that the manufacturer was not required to do bookkeeping, legally approved, or anything else, competent administrations.

If the exhortation is relevant, valid, or qualified, a rehearsed person should be requested during the call. The Declaration of Principles, which the American Bar Association Committee and the Publishers and Associations Committee have accepted and supported. It is not appropriate to reproduce, copy, or distribute any portion of this report in either electronic methods or in the community written.

Recording this delivery is carefully disclaimed, and the ability of this report is not permitted until the distributor has written a license. All rights. All rights held. The data provided in this document is expressed in an honest and predictable way, like any risk, in so far as abstention or anything else, is a singular and articulate duty for the beneficiary peruser to use or mistreat any approaches, procedures or bearing contained within it.

No legal responsibility or blame shall be held against the distributor for any reparation, loss, or money-related misfortune because of the results, whether explicitly or implied. All copyrights not held by the distributor are asserted by individual authors. The details herein are solely for educational purposes and are all-inclusive.

The data was entered without a contract or acknowledgment of assurance. The marks used shall be without consent, and the distribution of the mark shall be without the consent or support of the proprietor of the mark. All trademarks and trademarks within this book are just for explanation and are held clearly by the owners, who are not associated with this record.

TABLE OF CONTENTS

INTRODUCTION

WHAT ARE SOCIAL SKILLS
- There are distinct advantages to having well developed social skills.
- Why Social Skills Are Important
- Examples Of Social Skills

HOW TO IMPROVE SOCIAL SKILLS
- Ways to Improve Social Skills and Make You Sociable Anytime

Most Important Social Skills You Can Have To Make A Great Social Life

SOCIAL ANXIETY
- Specific and Generalized Social Anxieties
- MASTER YOUR SOCIAL SKILLS

GOOD HABIT
- Good Habits To Have To Be More Successful In Life.

SELF AWARENESS
- What is Self-Awareness Theory?
- Proven Benefits of Self-Awareness
- Ways to Increase Your Self-Awareness
- Tips for Improving Self-Awareness in Relationships

SOCIAL INFLUENCE
- Conformity / Majority Influence
- Social Change

CREATE AN EFFECTIVE GROUP OF CONVERSATION
- Significant Communication Skills Group

CHANGE YOUR MIND
- When Is a Cause Not a Cause?
- Key Steps to Changing Your Mind

OVERCOME YOUR DARK SIDE
- What Does Your Dark Side Really Mean?
- What Are You Supposed to Do with Your Dark Side?
- How Can You Accept Your Dark Side?
- How do you confront your dark side?
- How to Know When you've Made It

MANIPULATION
- Mental Health Effects Of Manipulation
- MANIPULATION IN RELATIONSHIPS

- EXAMPLES OF MANIPULATIVE BEHAVIOR
  - How To Spot Manipulation
  - Manipulative Tactics
  - Emotional Blackmail
  - Codependency
  - Passive-aggression
  - How To Deal With Manipulative People
- SOCIAL INTELLIGENCE AT WORK
  - Reasons why social intelligence matters at work
  - What Abilities Does Social Intelligence Convey?
  - Why Is Social Intelligence Necessary For Education And Future Jobs?
- HOW TO STOP PROCRASTINATION
  - Is Procrastination the Same as Being Lazy?
  - How To Overcome Procrastination
  - Work Out WHY you're Procrastinating
  - Adopt Anti-Procrastination Strategies
- CURE YOUR RELATIONSHIP
  - HEAR—To Hear Your Partner, Stay Present and Listen
  - EMPATHIZE—Allow Your Partner's Experience to Deeply Affect You
  - ACT—Take Action to Address Concerns and Show Willingness to Change
  - LOVE—Feel and Express Unconditional Love
- HOW TO INFLUENCE PEOPLE
  - Which Influence Tactic Is Right For You?
- HOW TO ANALYZE PEOPLE
  - Techniques in the Art of Reading People
- HOW TO MAKE FRIEND
  - Here Are Personal Tips To Get New Friends:
  - PRACTICAL MINDFULNESS
- BODY LANGUAGE
  - How to Read Negative Body Language
  - How to Project Positive Body Language
- DARK PSYCHOLOGY
- MIND CONTROL
- CONCLUSION

INTRODUCTION

From the time we're really young, we start learning the basics of social skills that are: learning how to live with, interacting with, and getting along with the people around you. If you have siblings, those basic skills come into play very quickly; sharing toys with a brother or sister and sharing a room. Those skills become much more important as we grow older and start school, as you now have to share with many more people. It may be difficult for children who have not been properly prepared for such an occurrence to adapt to this new society they have become a part of.

Many people who don't have socializing skills will normally look for advice from those people who know them. Peers and colleagues typically play a major role in strengthening an individual's socializing skills that are missing.

What works in one culture doesn't necessarily work in another; basic social skills are imperative to live a happy and enjoyable life in your community, workplace and home life, among others. It's the way we interact and conduct ourselves within society, in a nutshell; what's right and what's wrong in the society you're living in.

In order to fit in, society requires each person to behave in a manner that is not contrary to social norms. Being rude to another human, cursing in public, disrespectful conduct are all signs of not having the right social skills. Most people develop these skills early in life and progress into adult life; nevertheless, there are those who seem to follow the grain of society and lack the social skills that most of us don't even have to worry about; we just know how to behave properly. There are also people who have a clear understanding of this definition, but who are not sure how to develop their social skills in public situations.

When employers interview people, they're not just looking at their qualifications; they're assessing how they communicate with the employer. They search for signs and ask questions about certain subjects involving social interaction to see if the person interviewed has a clear understanding of social skills as to how to cope with a delicate situation. The lack of such skills may make a difference in getting a job or not; one must be able to conduct oneself professionally and politely in one's workplace and in society, among others.

WHAT ARE SOCIAL SKILLS

Social skills are the abilities that we use to communicate and connect with each other, both verbally and non-verbally, through expressions, body language and our personal appearance.
Human beings are sociable people, and we have evolved many ways to express our messages, opinions and feelings to others.

What is said is influenced by both spoken language and the way we say it, the tone of voice, the speed of speech and the phrases we say, as well as by more subtle signals such as body language, gestures and other non-verbal means of communication.
The fact that some people are better 'social integrators' than others has led to a detailed study of the meaning and interpersonal interaction.
Developing social skills is about becoming mindful of how we communicate with others, the messages we send, and how we can develop communication strategies to make communication more productive and successful.

There are distinct advantages to having well developed social skills.

1. More and Better Relationships
Interacting well with others leads to more relationships and, at times, friendships.

By improving your social skills, you become more confident, more attractive. People are more interested in charismatic people, while charismatic people are (or at least seem to be) more interested in them.

Most people know that you can't go far in life without good interpersonal relationships. Focusing on relationships will help you get a job, promote yourself, and make new friends. Well-honored social skills will improve your happiness and satisfaction and give you a better outlook on life.

More relationships can also help reduce the negative effects of stress and boost your self-esteem.

2. Better Communication

Communicating with others and being able to function in large groups naturally improves one's communication skills.

After all, you can't have great social skills without good communication skills, and being able to convey your thoughts and ideas can be the single most important skill you can improve in life.

3. Greater Efficiency

If you're good with people, it's easier to stop being around people who you don't like as much as others.

Some people dislike social interactions because they do not want to spend time with individuals who do not have similar values and views. It's a lot easier to attend a meeting at work or a party in your personal life if you know at least some of the people who are going to be there.

If you're in a social situation and don't want to spend time with 'John' because you don't like him or he can't support you with a specific problem, a strong set of social skills would enable you to respectfully express that you need to spend time with other people.

4. Advancing Career Prospects

The most desirable careers have a 'people aspect', and the most lucrative positions also require a significant amount of time spent engaging with staff, media and colleagues.

It is uncommon for a person to remain isolated in their office and yet excel in their work. Many organizations are searching for individuals with a clear, tactical, skillset: the ability to work together as a team and to influence and inspire people to do things.

5. Increased Overall Happiness

Getting along and understanding people will help to open a number of personal and career-related doors.

Having the courage to start a conversation at a work-related conference will lead to a new job offer with a higher salary. A smile and 'hello' in a social situation can lead to the formation of friendships.

Why Social Skills Are Important

Social skills are important because they help you create, sustain and establish relationships with colleagues, clients and new people alike. They are necessary to retain and develop regardless of your role, industry or level of experience.

Investing in relationships is beneficial for your career in many ways, some of which include:

- Obtaining ideas, information, techniques and perspectives from people with different areas of expertise.

- Providing your own viewpoint to the good of others.

- Achieving assignments and working together towards a shared goal.

- Provide mutual support for situations that are difficult or difficult to navigate.

- Expand the network in order to learn about and pursue new opportunities.

- Earning reviews and recommendations from people who can directly testify to your job, skills and qualities (and for whom you can do the same thing).

- Make the workplace more fun.

It is also important to demonstrate your social skills during the hiring process. Being able to work well and develop partnerships with others is a key quality employer to look for in candidates. It can also demonstrate your fitness for the culture of your business.

To explain social skills in your cover letter, give an example of how long you have collaborated with others to accomplish a goal that has brought success to your team or company. On your resume, list unique, observable accomplishments so you can expand on how you used your social skills to do so during your interview. During the interview, use the STAR approach for behavioral interview questions to clarify the occasions when social skills have been successful.

Examples Of Social Skills

Here are a few examples of qualities you can build to increase your social skills:
1. Effective communication
The main social skill is the ability to interact efficiently with others. If you have good communication skills, you will be able to communicate your opinions and ideas easily with others. Efficient communicators make good leaders since they can quickly describe programs and priorities in an easy-to-understand manner.

2. Conflict resolution
Disagreements and disappointment can occur in any situation. Conflict resolution is the opportunity to approach the root of the problem and find a workable solution. If you have strong conflict resolution skills, you may be well-suited to a position in HR where you can deal with conflicts between employees. You can also enjoy a position in customer service where you settle disputes with clients regarding the goods, services or policies of an organization.

3. Active listening
Active listening is the ability to pay close attention to the person who interacts with you. Productive listeners are generally well-respected by their peers because of the consideration and appreciation that others offer. You will improve your listening skills by concentrating on the speaker, avoiding distractions, and planning questions, suggestions or ideas to reply.

4. Empathy
Empathy is the desire to consider and connect with other people's emotions. If you are sympathetic, people will be more likely to believe you. Being more empathetic takes a deliberate effort to think more about how others feel. If you strengthen your compassion and friendship with others, you will be able to create deeper relationships that can be helpful in many ways.

5. Relationship management
Relationship management is the ability to sustain and build key relationships. For example, if you have a job in customer service, you may be responsible for managing the relationship between your company and a specific set of clients. Organizational executives maintain ties with stakeholders and investors. This is a useful social ability in a variety of roles.

6. Respect
Knowing when to initiate contact and respond is a crucial element of respect. In a team or community environment, allowing others to talk without interruption is seen as a required communication ability linked to respectfulness. Respectfully interacting often means using your time wisely with someone else staying on the subject, asking straightforward questions, and responding fully to any questions you have asked.

HOW TO IMPROVE SOCIAL SKILLS

There are several ways to improve your social skills. Here are just a few ways you can begin:

- Get your reviews. It may be helpful to ask trusted friends, advisors or managers to provide you with honest feedback on your areas of improvement. Use this input to start setting realistic goals for a solid, well-rounded collection of social skills.

- Set the objectives. Once areas for development have been established, use the SMART objectives system to work towards improving interpersonal skills in a clear, measurable manner.

- Find your money. There are endless courses, guides, books and more, both online and offline. Although you can probably pay for an e-book or lesson, there are also a lot of free tools that you can use. You will also find focused tools on subjects such as body language or negotiation.

- Identify areas of practice. When you've mastered strategies and tips to develop your social skills, put them into practice at home and at work. You can also search for volunteer opportunities or extra-curricular activities where you can develop interpersonal skills with less strain.

If you're looking for soft skills that will boost your employability and help you succeed in almost any career, social skills are a great place to start. The best way to develop your social skills is to put your learning in motion. A history that shows success with social skills can serve you well in many aspects of life.

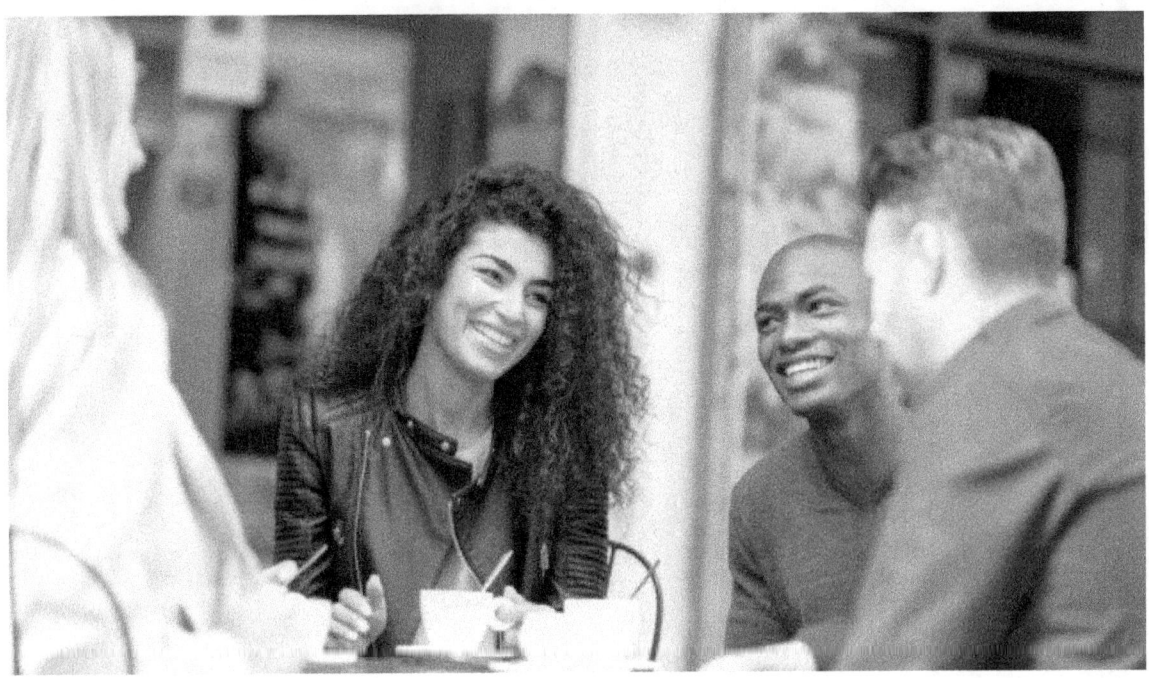

Ways to Improve Social Skills and Make You Sociable Anytime

If you feel like you're an awkward person at social events or you're unable to engage in conversations because you're shy, it can have an effect on your social life and career. However, you should start developing your social skills by adopting these techniques, and soon you'll be able to engage in positive conversations.

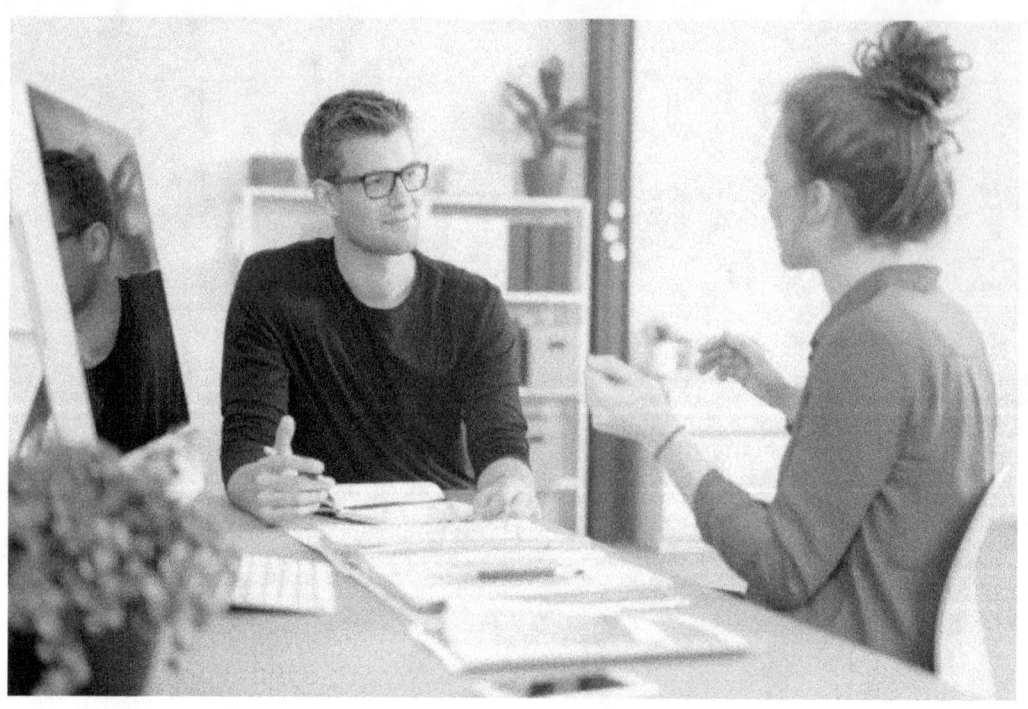

Behave Like a Social Person

You should act like a more social creature, even if you don't feel that way.
Don't let fear hold you back. Make a decision to speak to new people and engage in conversations even when you're anxious about it.
With time, it will be simpler, and you will soon begin to improve your social skills.

Start Small if Necessary

If it feels daunting to go to a party or spend time in a crowd, start small.
Go to the grocery store and say, "Thank you," to the clerk or go to the restaurant and order your dinner. Practice gradually.

Ask Open-Ended Questions

If you want your time in a discussion, get acquainted with open-ended questions. Encourage them to talk so that you don't have to make idle chit-chat.
Ask questions that require more than a yes or no answer, and you may open the door to ask the other person to keep the conversation going.

Encourage Others to Talk about Themselves

Many of the people just like talking about themselves. Ask a question about the profession, hobbies, or family of an individual. Show that you're interested in hearing what's being said.
If you want to keep the conversation going, you're supposed to make it like playing ping pong.

Create Goals for Yourself

Place some small goals for yourself. You may want to learn one specific skill, or you might want to start a social activity in your neighborhood.
Set a goal and start working on plans that will improve your social life.

Offer Compliments Generously

Compliments may be a perfect way to open the door to a discussion. Give your coworker a compliment on a presentation he gave at a meeting or compliment your neighbor on his new car.
Compliments will show people that you are cool, and there are more reasons why you should pay a compliment to someone every day.

Read Books about Social Skills

There are a lot of books on the market that can help you learn specific social skills and ways to start conversations.
Bear in mind, though, that reading about these skills is not going to make you an expert. You're going to have to practice them over and over again.

Practice Good Manners

Good manners go a long way towards improving social skills. Practice being respectful and using good manners at the table.

Pay Attention to Your Body Language

Non-verbal contact is of great significance. Pay attention to the type of body language you're using.
Try to appear relaxed, make an appropriate amount of eye contact and appear to be open to conversation.

Join a Social Skills Support Group

Many communities offer support groups for social skills. Support groups encourage people who feel nervous, uncomfortable, or incredibly anxious about social situations to learn and practice new skills.
You're going to start developing social skills, and maybe you're going to be able to make new friends who understand your difficulties.

Stay Up to Date on Current Events

Catch up on emerging events and news reports, so you've got something to talk to people about.
Try to avoid something that is too divisive, such as politics, but speak about other news items that might be of interest.
It can be a perfect way to start a conversation, and it can help you stick to neutral subjects.

Identify and Replace Negative Thoughts

If you have a lot of pessimistic feelings about your social experiences, it may be a self-fulfilling prophecy.
For example, a person who thinks, "I'm very uncomfortable, and I'm going to embarrass myself," might be sitting in the corner at a party. As a result, he might leave the party, thinking that he must be very uncomfortable because no one has spoken to him.

Identify negative feelings that are likely to drag you down. Replace them with more rational thoughts like, "I can make a conversation, and I can meet new people." Don't allow yourself to linger on thoughts that are not positive.

Most Important Social Skills You Can Have To Make A Great Social Life

You know, as a life hacker, that some of your acts are responsible for much of your success. Some social skills make the most of the difference when it comes to making friends and maintaining a great social life. There are six of them here.

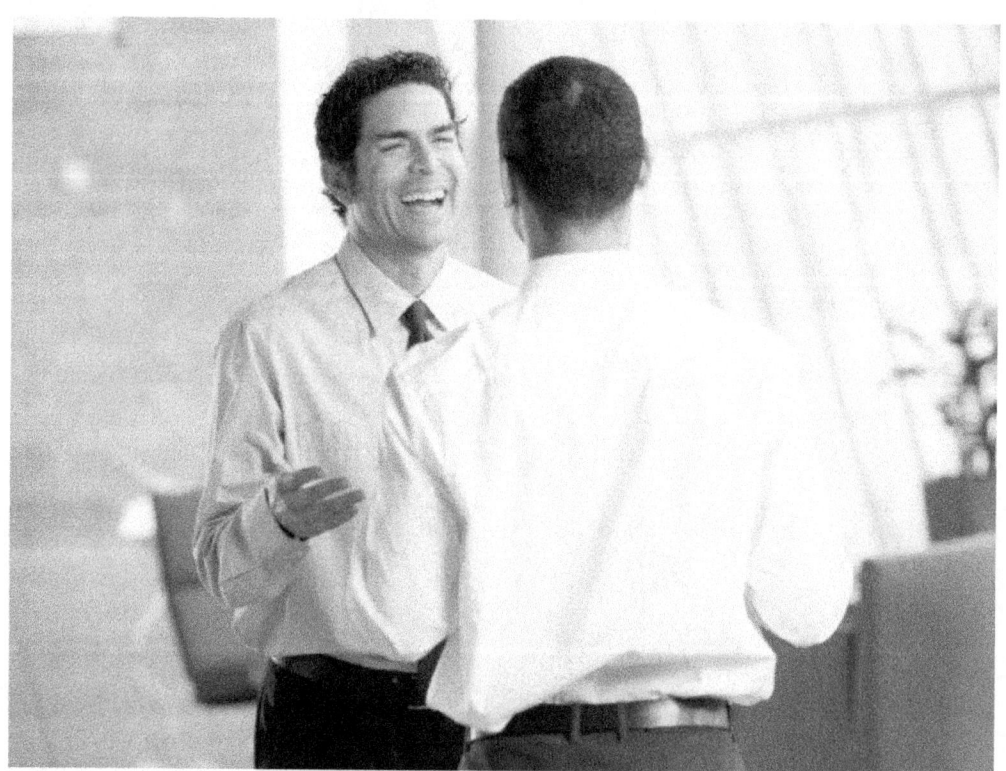

1. Find Great Places to Meet New People

Friendship is always going to happen in a certain setting. This setting may be a school, a workplace, or just a friend's house. It often begins with a situation that brings people together. Much of this happens by chance, and that's far from ideal.
If you want a great social life, it's easier to take care of this and find fun ways to meet new people. I suggest that you find private spaces such as local societies or social clubs for your interests. As a rule of thumb, you need to find areas where it's easy to go up to a stranger and introduce yourself.

2. Select the Right People

If you meet someone new and like them, you need to know if they're ready for a new relationship. Some people just have too many friends, and some are going through a stressful event, and they can't find the time to be social.
You better not take this as a refusal; they just don't have time to be friends.
If you want to find out if they're ready for friendship, try and find out if they're socially active. You can do that in two ways: first, you can ask where they're going, and second, you can pay attention to what they're going through in their lives. If someone is about to move, change jobs, get married or have a child, you can be sure they won't have time to hang out.

3. Spot Commonalities with Others

A common mistake people make when they encounter new friends is to concentrate on how different the other person is from them. They start pointing out differences of opinion as a way to prove how special they are. It's a good thing to be special, but it shouldn't keep you from communicating with potential mates.
Instead, you should look for parallels in views, attitudes, priorities, and desires. That's going to give you a little common ground, so you can establish friendship if you want to. You can always disagree with them, and even taunt them once they become friends with you.

4. Show Little Vulnerabilities Early On

That sounds more dangerous than it really is. If you're going to be friends with someone, there's a degree of confidence that needs to be established; both of you have to make certain things clear to each other.
To kick-start friendship, there is a degree of trust that needs to be established. Even when you're just getting to know someone, there's a need for a sense of "we can trust each other."
You don't have to share the big secrets of your life. All you've got to do is be a little more available. The rule of thumb is to be 5% more opens than average. When you do so, you will see that the other person is more likely to do the same thing; they, too, can show some weakness. These might be odd or amusing habits or the peculiarities of each one of you. It plays a major part in the process of friendship, but most people are not even aware of it.

5. Show Others That You Like Them

The first time you meet someone, you both have to like each other to become friends. This completely subjective part of the first experiences does not scare you. What you should do here is always believe that you're going to be accepted and that you would want to meet new people.
When you keep these two minds, you immediately begin to act in a way that indicates to others that you like them, which makes them like you. This is a self-fulfilling prophecy: if they think you like them, they'll start to love you.

6. Treat Making Friends as a Skill

Ironically, socially successful people never quit talking about friendship and making friends. Socially unsuccessful people, on the other hand, believe it's something you're either born with or not.
It's true that some of us knew this very well at a young age. And others, including me, had to find it out a little later. As with any other skill, there are concepts and techniques that anyone can learn. The good news is that you can only get better when you start studying.

SOCIAL ANXIETY

We all know the feeling of being anxious or awkward in a social setting. You may have cried out when you met someone new or had sweaty palms before you made a major presentation. Public speaking or going into a stranger's space is not necessarily fun for anyone, but most people will get through it.

Social anxiety is the fear of being viewed and perceived negatively by others, leading to feelings of inadequacy, inferiority, self-consciousness, shame, humiliation, and depression.

If a person normally becomes (irrationally) nervous in social settings, but tends to be better off when he or she is alone, then "social anxiety" may be a concern.

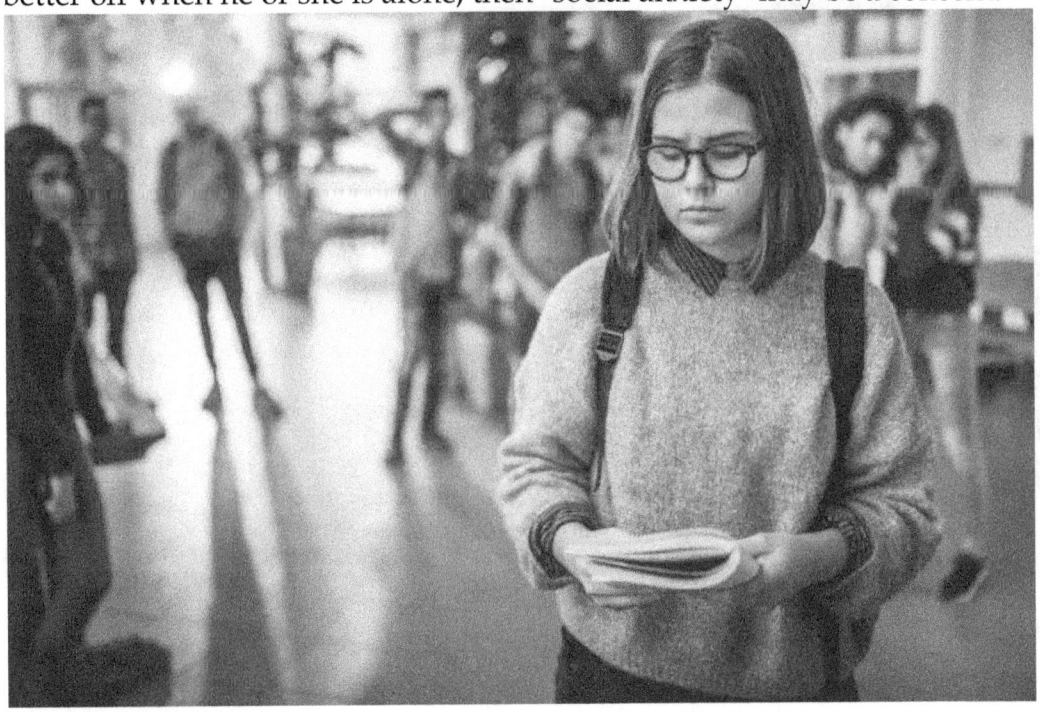

The Third Largest Mental Health Care Problem

Social anxiety disorder (formerly referred to as "social phobia") is a much more common problem than previous estimates have led us to believe. Millions of people around the world suffer from this devastating and traumatic condition every day, either from specific social anxieties or from more widespread ones.

In the United States, epidemiological studies have recently identified social anxiety disorder as the country's third-largest psychological disorder after depression and alcoholism. It is estimated that about 7% of the population currently suffers from some form of social anxiety. The lifetime prevalence rate for developing social anxiety disorder is 13-14%.

Specific and Generalized Social Anxieties

Specific social anxiety would be the fear of speaking (only) in front of groups, while people with generalized social anxiety are anxious, nervous, and uncomfortable in almost all social situations.

It is much more common for people with social anxieties to have a generalized type of disorder. When anticipatory anxiety, worry, indecision, depression, embarrassment, inferiority and self-denial are involved in most life situations, a generalized form of social anxiety is at work.

Symptoms of Social Anxiety Disorder

People with social anxiety disorder usually experience significant emotional distress in the following situations:

- To be introduced to other people.
- To be teased or criticized.
- To be the center of attention.
- To be watched while doing something.

- I am meeting people in authority ('important people').
- Most of the social encounters, especially with strangers.
- Going around the room (or table) in a circle and having to say something about themselves.
- Interpersonal relationships, be they friendships or romantic relationships.

This list is certainly not a complete list of symptoms — other feelings have also been linked to social anxiety.

Physiological manifestations that accompany social anxiety may include intense fear, racing of the heart, turning red or blushing, excessive sweating, dry throat and mouth, trembling (fear of taking a glass of water or eating utensils), difficulty swallowing, and muscle twitching, especially around the face and neck.

Constant, intense anxiety that doesn't go away is the most common feature.

People with a social anxiety disorder know that their anxiety is irrational and does not make sense (i.e. cognitive) rationally. However, "knowing" something is not the same thing as "believe" or "feeling" something.

Thus, for people with social anxieties, thoughts and feelings of anxiety persist and show no signs of going away — despite the fact that people with social anxieties "face their fears" every day of their lives.

The Most Important Elements In Overcoming Social Anxiety

1. Awareness and understanding of the problem;
2. A commitment to carry out cognitive-behavioral therapy even when it is repetitive and seems difficult;
3. Practice, practice, practice to get that information (i.e. cognitive methods, strategies, and concepts) deep into your brain-so that these cognitive methods become routine and automatic;
4. Participate in a social anxiety therapy group in which you can work slowly and gradually on problems that cause anxiety in the real world.

That is, the person who is anxious to read in public uses specific strategies to meet his or her goal, while the person who wants to learn how to make introductions and engage in small conversations during social activities is slowly working towards his or her goals.

We use role-playing, acting, tape recorder and video camera, question and answer periods, mock job interviews, and do foolish things deliberately as part of our behavioral therapy group for people with social anxieties.

Note: The ladder or "hierarchy" should be used as a flexible guide for planning. We want to practice, to meet our goals, to move up our expectations, to meet our objectives, and to move up our expectations until our goal is finally met.

MASTER YOUR SOCIAL SKILLS

Let's face it, not all of us score an "A" when it comes to sociability and friendliness. Indeed, many people tremble to the idea of attending a social gathering or networking event.

Unfortunately, they're inevitable at times.

Whether you're an introvert who's quickly drained into mandatory conversations, or would never call yourself a "people-to-people," there are behavioral hacks that trigger relationships and positive reactions from others.

Here are social techniques, some of which are supported by studies that will ensure your next social interaction.

1. Show your palms

You'd assume that the eyes are the first place you're looking for when you meet someone, but they're your hands. It's an evolutionary behavior that still persists; a survival mechanism that ensures that the other person does not carry weapons.
So, if you meet someone for the first time, keeping your hands visible and showing your palms will make them comfortable.

2. Use their name

It's the sweetest sound in everybody's ears. Hearing your own name sparks parts of your brain. Using a person's name in a conversation, they'll take their interest and put a smile on their faces. We're not supposed to make a note that it's too much to use in every sentence.
"In two months, you can make more friends by becoming more interested in people than you can in two years, trying to get other people interested in you."

3. Original questions

If you want to ensure a boring conversation, ask, "So, what are you doing for a living? "It's so worn out, yet the textbook approach to every conversation is still so common. Charisma coach JT Tran asks, "If you were a pizza topping, what would you be?" The new questions will always evoke a smile and interesting conversations.

4. Vary your tone

Charismatic speakers always adjust their voice tone. Think back to that painfully boring lecture, the professor was monotonous right? Varying the tone of your conversation will keep the other person engaged and interested in you.

5. Hand gestures

A survey of 760 people who rated and watched Ted Talks for hundreds of hours revealed a direct relationship between the number of views and the number of hand gestures.
The top Ted Talks, which averaged more than 7 million views, used twice as many hand gestures as the ones that averaged over 100 K views.
Why are people attracted by hand gestures? You talk to them on two levels: verbal and non-verbal.

6. The slight touch

The line between creepy and effective is very thin. The highly charismatic Bill Clinton is a master of strategic social touch. Whether it's a pat on the back or a touch of the elbow, when you're done in the right moment, your relationship with a person can actually become better.

7. Stand side-on

Standing in front of a person can be perceived as confrontational. You can adjust your position as the conversation continues, but initially standing slightly sideways will ensure that the interaction starts on the best foot.
"Talk to someone about themselves, and they're going to listen for hours."

8. Eye contact

Psychologists at Aberdeen University found that people were more attracted to the faces that maintained eye contact than to those who turned away from their eyes.
Of course, intense eye contact would make anyone uncomfortable. However, maintaining a consistent amount will enhance likability and attractiveness.

9. Smile

Last but certainly not least. There is a social obligation that comes with a smile, and rarely does it go unreciprocated. The release of happy chemicals comes with a smile. Those happy chemicals are going to make it hard for someone not to like you.

GOOD HABIT

Habits are behaviors and patterns that you show by default. They allow you to carry out important activities, such as taking a shower, brushing your teeth, getting ready for work.

Interestingly, every day, you follow this routine without considering it. Your unconscious habits make room for your brain to perform more advanced activities, such as problem-solving and choosing what book to read.

Everyone has habits, and several of those habits are activated every day. I would classify them into three groups:

- The first category includes habits that you hardly notice as they have become a major part of your life, such as brushing your teeth or wearing clothes.

- The second category includes good habits of having to be more successfullike: eating healthy, exercising your body and reading books.

- The last group consists of those habits that are harmfullike: procrastination, smoking or overeating.

Habits are essential to the success of life or to the likely end of failure. Yet, as important as habits are, some lack the knowledge of their capabilities.

Habits are the default activities you engage in without giving an afterthought. They're automatic behavioral or mental activities. They help you do some things without exerting too much energy. They're simplifying your life.

Several people are trying to break bad habits. Some people diet to stop overeating, for example. Habits can hinder or affect your performance and productivity.

Good Habits To Have To Be More Successful In Life.

1. Begin Your Day with Meditation

Early in the morning, I recommend thoughtful meditation. This practice helps you to be at the moment. As a result, you can be mindful of challenging situations during the day. Different stressors may trigger as you go through the day; meditation helps you to remain calm before you face the challenges.
Personally, it helps me to come up with strategies and think about ideas. Meditation is a good habit to have if you want to be connected to what is important in your life.

2. Be Grateful for What You Have

Sometimes you waste your time thinking about what's not enough. You are immersed in these daunting challenges. But the challenges justify the presence of hope. You have expectations when you have a life. When you're six feet below, you'll be free from challenges. The only strategy you need to stop focusing on your problems is to focus on what you've got.
Gratitude is a time-tested path to success, health and happiness. It's going to redirect your focus to what you've got from what you lack. Here's what James Clear is doing every day,
"One thing I say is that I am grateful for every day I sit down to eat dinner."

3. Smile

Can you pause and smile before you continue reading this?
Now here's what's just happened on the basis of research conducted by the Psychological Sciences Association; you set a pace for a happy life when you smile. A genuine smile, or what is called a Duchenne smile, is a good habit to have if you want to find spiritual, emotional, and mental peace of mind.
Smiling induces the release of molecules that work to combat stress. The physiological state of your body is what determines the state of your mind. When you slouch or frown, your mind takes notes of unhappiness and depression. But once you adjust yourself with a smile, you start to feel a new level of excitement and vibrancy.
Can you smile again?

4. Start Your Day with a Healthy Breakfast

Starting your day with a healthy breakfast is a good habit to have and is a crucial part of your life. However, about 31 million Americans skip breakfast every day.
If you're fed up hearing that breakfast is a crucial part of your day, you're only fighting the truth. If you want to be more successful, you need to 'breakfast' with healthy foods every morning.
This habit is not difficult to form if you usually run out of the door every single morning. You can wake up earlier to fix your own meal so that you won't break down during the day.

5. Exercise Daily

One of the good habits you should have is to exercise your body and muscles every day. You're not going to have to run a marathon or liftweights. All you need to do is engage in less strenuous activities that oxygenate your blood and inject endorphins into your body. Jack Dorsey, CEO of Twitter, has classified exercise as a good habit of maximizing his already jam-packed schedule. He said,
'I wake up at 5 a.m., meditate for 30 minutes, 7-minute workout 3 times, make coffee and check-in.'
He said on Product Hunt that he follows this routine every day as it gives him a steady-state that empowers him to be more productive.

6. Manage Your Time as You Manage Your Finance

Another good habit is to manage your time effectively. This goes a long way to having an impact on your achievement.
Time management is what separates the successful from the rest of the world as we all have the same amount of time. How you leverage time determines your potential to be successful in life.
So How Do You Manage Your Time Effectively?
Here's Jack Dorsey's recommendation in one of the Technology events;
"I perform effective time management by the theme of my days and practice self-discipline. These themes help me deal with distractions and interactions. If that day's request or task is not aligned with the theme, I don't do it. This sets a pace for everyone in the company to deliver and evaluate their progress.
And this is Dorsey's weekly theme:

- Monday, management.
- Tuesdays – Product, please.
- Wednesday, marketing and growth.
- Thursdays – Developers and Partners.
- Fridays – culture and recruitment.
- Saturdays, take off.
- Sundays – Reflection, feedback, strategy and preparation for Monday.

No wonder he was able to run two companies when others were struggling with one job.

7. Set Daily Goals with Intentions

Everybody's got goals. It may be related to a business or a personal life. The truth is, we all tend towards one direction or another. However, while long-term goals can give you direction, it is your daily goals that you set that will help you develop short-term goals that are essential to your success.

Long-term goals may not give you the motivation you need to keep up with. But when you implement your short-term milestones on a daily basis, you get fired up, and you can overcome the challenges that come with taking on larger tasks.

Here's the main truth: Successful people don't set goals without setting their intentions. According to Forbes' Jennifer Cohen,

"What helps you to achieve your desired expectations is to ensure that your daily goals are accompanied by your intentions."

Be mindful of your daily goals!

8. Seek Inspiration

It's usually hard to be inspired for a considerable amount of time. Sometimes, you get discouraged and feel like you're giving up on your goals when things don't work out as intended.

A practical approach to staying on top of the situation is to inspire you every day. When you wake up in the morning after meditation, watch some motivating videos and let the story of great leaders inspire you.

Set up what Anthony Robbins called the 'hour of power.' Determine how many minutes you spend, but make it count. Inspiration is the fuel for achievement because if you can conceive it in your mind, you can do it.

Michal Solowow, an investor and founder of Mitex, a construction company, put it this way.

"The problems I encounter in my everyday life motivate me to find solutions. This is a self-propelled mechanism. It was never a motivating factor to become a billionaire."

9. Save Steadily, Invest with All Prudence

I can't exhaust the good habits I have without talking about saving and investing. Most of the time, when you live in your present moment, you overlook the significance of saving for the future. According to CNBC, an emergency of $1000 will push several Americans into debt.

But it's not enough to save, and you need to invest your fund and be wise with it. If you pay attention to this now, you're going to set yourself up for a successful life in the future. Ensure that you save at least six months in your emergency account so that you can be prepared for any future emergencies.

10. Budget and Track Your Spendings

Benjamin Franklin warned against taking care of small expenses. He said,
"A small leak sinks a big ship."
It's easy to discard small expenses, but the truth is that they always add up. This happens when you don't have a budget.
Budgeting is a good habit that can have a significant impact on your financial life. The money that you spend on extravagant lifestyles can be saved and invested in your future.

Try to cultivate these good habits and it will make you more successful as you go through life. The quicker you cultivate them, the faster you achieve your goals.

SELF AWARENESS

Self-awareness is the ability to see oneself clearly and objectively through reflection and introspection.

While it may not be possible to achieve total objectivity about oneself (this is a debate that continues to rage throughout the history of philosophy), there are certainly degrees of self-awareness. It's on the spectrum.

Although everyone has a fundamental idea of what self-awareness is.

What is Self-Awareness Theory?

The theory of self-awareness is based on the idea that you are not your thoughts, but the entity observing your thoughts; you are the thinker, separate and apart from your thoughts.

We can go about our day without giving our inner self any extra thought, just thinking and feeling and acting as we will; but we can also focus our attention on that inner self, the ability that Duval and Wicklund called "self-assessment."

When we engage in self-assessment, we can give some thought to whether we think and feel and act as we "should" or follow our standards and values. We do this every day, using these standards as a way to judge the correctness of our thoughts and behavior.

Using these standards is a key component of self-control, as we evaluate and determine whether we make the right choices to achieve our objectives.

Proven Benefits of Self-Awareness

Now, let's turn our attention to research on the results of self-awareness.

As you might imagine, there are many benefits to the practice of self-awareness:

- It can make us more proactive, enhance our acceptance and encourage positive self-development.

- Self-awareness enables us to see things from the perspective of others, to practice self-control, to work creatively and productively, and to experience pride in ourselves and our work as well as general self-esteem.

- This leads to better decision making.

- It can make us better at work, better communicators at work, and enhance self-confidence and job-related well-being.

The benefits listed are enough to start working towards improving self-awareness, but this list is by no means exhaustive. Self-awareness has the potential to enhance virtually every experience you have, as it is a tool and practice that can be used anywhere, at any time, to ground yourself in a moment, to assess yourself and the situation realistically, and to help you make good choices.

Ways to Increase Your Self-Awareness

We now have some clear examples of self-awareness in mind. We know how to accept self-awareness and evolve. But how are you going to do that? What did our leading characters do to exercise self-awareness?

There are many ways to build and practice self-awareness, but here are some of the most effective:

1. Practice Mindfulness and Meditation

Mindfulness means being present at the moment and paying attention to yourself and the surroundings instead of being lost in thought or rumination or daydreaming.
Meditation is a practice of focusing your attention on something like your pulse, mantra, or feeling and letting your thoughts drift away, rather than holding on to it.
Both activities will help you become more aware of your internal state and of your responses to things. They can also help you identify your thoughts and feelings and keep you from getting so caught up in them that you lose your grasp on your "self."

2. Practice Yoga

Yoga is a physical exercise, but it's just as much of mental practice. When your body is stretching, bending, and flexing, your mind is gaining discipline, self-acceptance, and mindfulness. You become more aware of your body and all the emotions that manifest, and you become more aware of your mind and the thoughts that arise.

You can even combine yoga with mindfulness or meditation to improve your self-awareness.

3. Make Time to Reflect

Reflection can be done in multiple ways (including diary; see the next tip) and is flexible to the reflective person, but the important thing is to go through your thoughts, feelings, and behaviors to see where you reached your goals, where you missed them, and where you could change.
You can also think about your own values and see if they are sufficient for you to hang on to. You can try writing in a book, speaking out loud, or just sit back and relax, whatever makes you think about yourself.

4. Journaling

The advantage of journaling is that it allows you to identify, clarify and accept your thoughts and feelings. It helps you to find out what you want, what you need, and what works for you. It can also help you find out what you don't want, what isn't important to you, and what doesn't work for you.
They're both equally important to learn. Whether you like to write free-flowing posts, bulleted lists, or poems, writing your thoughts and feelings allows you to become more conscious and deliberate.

5. Ask the people you love

It's important to feel like we know ourselves from inside, but external feedback is also beneficial. Ask your family and your close friends what they're thinking about you. Make them inform you and see what the real rings are with you and what shocks you.
Carefully consider what they're doing, and think about it when you're journaling or otherwise thinking. Of course, don't take the word of one person as gospel; you need to speak to a number of people to get a detailed view of yourself.
And note, at the end of the day, it's your self-confidence and emotions that matter most to you!

Tips for Improving Self-Awareness in Relationships

If you want to support your clients with their relationship problems, here are some excellent tips for incorporating more self-awareness within the context of a relationship:

- Practice mindfulness, particularly when you communicate with your loved ones. Pay attention to the words they utter, their speech, their body language, and their facial expressions. We always convey far more detail to the latter three than we do to our own terms. Give all your attention to your loved ones.

- Have regular discussions on the relationship. It's important to keep things in perspective and make sure nothing falls between cracks. When you have regular conversations about your relationship with your loved ones, it's a lot harder to avoid or ignore things that can develop into issues. It also lets you focus on your part and get ready to discuss your emotions, feelings, and behavior with your loved ones.

- Spend quality time together and separately. This is particularly important for romantic relationships, as we often find ourselves spending most or all of our free time with our spouse or partner. However, as much as you love and enjoy spending time with your partner, everyone needs some quality time on their own.

Make sure you and your partner both have some "me" quality time to think about what you want, what you need, and what your goals are. This will help keep you from integrating too much into your partner and preserving your individuality and security. Then, as there will be two independent, stable and balanced adults in the relationship, it will be even more rewarding and fulfilling for both partners as they spend quality time together.

- Share your view and consider it theirs. It's easy to get too caught up in our perspective on things; but, in addition to our own, healthy relationships require us to consider the needs of others. To know what our loved ones need, and to meet those needs, we must first identify and understand them. We do this by practicing our self-awareness and sharing that knowledge with friends and family.

If you never check in with your loved ones about their views or thoughts, it can cause you to drift apart and prevent true, fulfilling intimacy. Ask your loved ones for their perspective and share your viewpoint with them.

In short, a little extra self-awareness can be of great benefit to anyone who wants to improve.

SOCIAL INFLUENCE

Social influence implies any non-coercive strategy, method, process or manipulation that relies on the social-psychological structure of the individual as a means of creating or altering the perception or behavior of the object, whether or not this attempt is based on the specific actions of the control agent or on the self-organizing nature of the social structures. It may be contrasted with two other forms of influence:

- Power or control of critical resources, including its most aggressive use of battle.

- Outright deceit to lead an organism to believe that it does X, when in fact it does something else. In other words, social manipulation uses tactics that cater to the social nature of the individual. Among humans, it is their nature to fear, to feel dissonance, to return favors, to appreciate what is scarce, to empathize with others, to make decisions based on context, to pursue imaginary goals, and to easily adopt the social roles of their social group along with other characteristics. Social influence strategies use these qualities of human nature to invoke such mechanisms as conformity (creating or changing behavior or opinion that corresponds to the response of others), persuasion or behavioral change (change in response to a message, debate or communication), enforcement (change in response to an explicit request), and surrender to social forces (change in response to the structure of a message)

Social influence is the process by which the attitudes, values or behavior of the individual are influenced by the presence or action of others. Conformity, obedience and minority control are three fields of social power.

Conformity / Majority Influence

Conformity is a type of social influence described as a change of belief or action in response to real or imagined social pressure. It's also known as majority influence.

Obedience

Obedience is a type of social influence in which a person follows an order from another person who is typically a figure of authority.

Resistance to Social Influence

Independent behavior is a concept used by psychologists to describe behavior that does not seem to be affected by others. This happens when a person resists the pressure to conform or obey.
- Locus of Control

The word 'Locus of Control' refers to how much power a person feels they have in their actions. An individual may have either an internal control locus or an external control locus.

People with a high internal control locus see themselves as having a great deal of personal influence over their actions and are therefore more likely to take responsibility for their behavior. I did well on the tests, for example, though I revised it extremely hard. A person with a high external control locus, on the other hand, perceives their behavior as a result of external influences or chance – e.g. I did well on the test because it was so simple.

Research has shown that people with an internal control locus appear to be less conforming and less compliant (i.e. more independent). Additionally, they are better at resisting external pressure to conform or comply, perhaps because they feel responsible for their actions.

Minority Influence

Minority control happens when a small group (minority) affects the opinion of a larger group (majority). This will happen if the minority behaves in the following ways.
- Consistency

Being consistent and unchanging is more likely to influence the majority than if the majority is unstable and changes their minds.
- Commitment

When the majority challenges someone with self-confidence and commitment to taking a common stance and refuses to back their own, they may believe that they have a point.
- Flexibility

A number of scholars have questioned whether continuity alone is necessary to influence the majority. They argue that the secret to this is how the majority interprets the truth. If a consistent minority is seen as rigid, uncompromising and dogmatic, it is unlikely to change the views of the majority. However, if they tend to be versatile and pragmatic, they are likely to be seen as less severe, more rational, more cooperative and fairer. As a result, they will have a better chance of changing the majority view.

Some researchers have gone further, suggesting that it is not just the appearance of flexibility and compromise that is important, but that it is actually flexibility and compromise. This possibility has been investigated by Nemeth.

Their trial was based on a simulated jury in which groups of three participants and one confederate had to decide on the amount of compensation to be paid to the victim of a ski-lift accident. If a strong minority protested for a very small sum and declined to change its stance, it has little effect on the majority. However, as it compromised and went some way towards a majority position, the majority changed their position.

Social Change

Social change happens when culture as a whole adopts a new belief or practice that is then widely accepted as a 'norm.' The processes of social power involved in social change include minority influence, internal control locus and resistance to authority.

Social change is usually the result of the influence of minorities. This is when a small group of people (minority) tries to convince the majority to follow their point of view. This often applies to individual action, since the minority resists pressure to conform and comply. Typically, the minority has an internal control center.

It has been noticed that as soon as the minority starts to educate people of their way of thinking, the snowball effect starts to happen. This means that more and more people take a minority view until the minority eventually becomes the majority. At this point, those who have not changed their opinion are a minority, and will often comply with the majority's view.

Social Influence Analysis

In order to understand the eusocial or social species and to predict the behavior of its members, it is essential to analyze the nature of the social impact within that species. Such an analysis of social influence consists of a description of the tactics of social influence used by members of the species, the concepts or psychological processes underlying those tactics (e.g. dissonance, principles of social cognition), how influence is shared within the community (e.g. likely tactics employed, profiling of influence agents), patterns of influence within the species and its societies.

Social Influence Determines Most Decisions People Make

Believe it or not, social influence has a greater impact on your decision-making than your conscious mind does. We all like to think that we are in control of all our decisions. We've also been pretty good at coming up with arguments (after the fact) to explain the choices we make and prove (to ourselves and others) that we're not under any other control. Or, as Benjamin Franklin said, "It's so easy to be a rational being because it enables one to find or create a justification for everything one has a mind to do."

Truth is the bulk of choices we make starting out of our consciousness. We're wired to look to others for behavioral cues as to how we're going to act in unfamiliar situations. Imagine that you grew up poor and were invited to a fancy dinner at the local country club. It's extremely unlikely that you're going to go to dinner and start belching and making offensive jokes. You'd be more likely to be worried about making yourself a fool, and you'd take as many clues as you can from the actions of others to direct your own. If you see two separate forks at your place setting, you'd probably try to see which one the others are using before digging into your salad.

That was a deliberate example of how we look at things before we make decisions. Now I'm going to demonstrate a few cases where people were not fully aware that their conduct was based on the circumstances around them.

Latest studies show that three-quarters of college students have been consuming alcohol, and almost 50 per cent have been binging. This has become a significant concern when more than 1,800 U.S. college students die every year from alcohol-related incidents, and more than 600,000 suffer alcohol-related injuries. Students see almost half of their peers binge drinking and think it's okay or natural, but the fact is that most students are not comfortable with their peers' drinking habits. So, while on the surface, most students seem to be cool with binge drinking; in fact, they are just succumbing to social pressure.

Another example is the two planes crashing into the building of the World Trade Center on September 11, 2001. Almost everyone on the 87th floor died because they all looked at each other in the wake of the accident to see how they responded, and the majority remained calm. Having everyone else doing their business made everybody realize there was no need to worry, including those who were originally scared. In the meantime, on the 88th floor, just one floor above them, a man named J.J. Augier ran around the building, ordering everyone to leave immediately. They've all come out alive.

If you are in a classroom setting, you can ask a relatively simple question as to whether or not two lines of equal length are of the same length. Then all you have to do is set things up so that the first few people you call say "NO" and then ask if there's someone who feels they're the same length of time. It is extremely unlikely that anyone would speak up and give the correct answer. If you ask first-year law students what kind of law they want to study, you'll get a wide range of answers. At the beginning of their second year, if you ask the same group the same question, you'll probably just get two or three different responses. It's not just a coincidence that people tend to take on the traits of those with whom they spend most of their time. This is the strength of the force of culture.

That's why culture is so important. It's the social atmosphere that defines people's behavior, not the rule. The social uproar against the dentist who killed Cecil the Lion is likely to keep more people from killing big animals than any rule we have on cards. Maybe we'd be much better off as a country if we avoided the knee-jerk reaction to create new legislation whenever we're faced with something we don't like and instead focus on social power to bring about positive change.

CREATE AN EFFECTIVE GROUP OF CONVERSATION

Before we talk about the various skills and practices that can be used to promote an atmosphere in which groups of all sizes interact well, let's first talk about some of the words that we will use in this lesson.

Group communication can be described as more than three-but less than 20-people who have a conversation. It varies from a dyad conversation, which is when two people have a face-to-face conversation. We're not going to waste much time learning about a dyad in this chapter.

Okay, well, we were all there. You are assigned to a group or team, and you need to collaborate and work together to achieve the desired result. Working in groups can be a nightmare if there is no good communication.

There always seems to be one or two people who do most of the work, whilst the other members of the team contribute the bare minimum. Many organizations understand these problems and collaborate with their Human Resources department to train staff to work more collaboratively.

Effective group communication may take place in many forms, but you will see the best results (especially in large groups) when there is a leader or facilitator in the conversation. It's not important, but it makes things a lot less stressful. Group members will gain and contribute more if they believe they are included in the discussion, and there is general respect among the participants in the conversation.

Some of the important things to look for when monitoring a group conversation are verbal and non-verbal cues. Non-verbal cues are the most important ones to look for because they are silent indicators of how people feel or interpret a message.

Examples of non-verbal cues include:

- When someone sits down.
- Gestures of the lips.
- Nuances in sound and style of voice.
- Touching the ears.

Other signals to be found may include written and interpersonal skills, or simple life skills that you use every day to interact with others. Good group communication is not all about talking.

Another factor that needs to be discussed is how the community is structured during the discussion. Sitting can play an important role in developing an atmosphere where people feel comfortable to express their thoughts. Organizing a group in a circle is the ideal form for the best interactions.

Significant Communication Skills Group

Good communication only happens when you send a direct message, and the message is interpreted and understood. Taking the time to learn the skills required to interact effectively will enable people to overcome their differences and create trust and respect. Everyone has places where they can work to develop their communication skills. Some of the most important things that a person can do to be an effective communicator are:

- Be a good listener to me.

- Be conscious in yourself and others of non-verbal signals.

- Keep your emotions and stress under control.

- Act with others to learn and empathize.

The perfect community climate doesn't happen immediately. To have a healthy atmosphere in which employees feel comfortable sharing their ideas and working together, work is needed, and it is only after confidence is established and teamwork is developed that the company will benefit from working together. Trust is, therefore, something that is important for people to work productively. Failure to trust can lead to a wedge between employees and build an atmosphere of hostility. Confidence is also focused on loyalty and the ability to depend on a coworker.

One activity that is a great way to build trust between peers and encourage them to assess their own, as well as the verbal and non-verbal communication difficulties of others, is to direct a blind person to certain items or to specific obstacles. This is how it works:

Many educators are scientifically aware of the importance of working in teams, groups or professional learning communities. Most of us want a healthy relationship with colleagues and a desire for the support, understanding and direction of others who walk in our shoes.

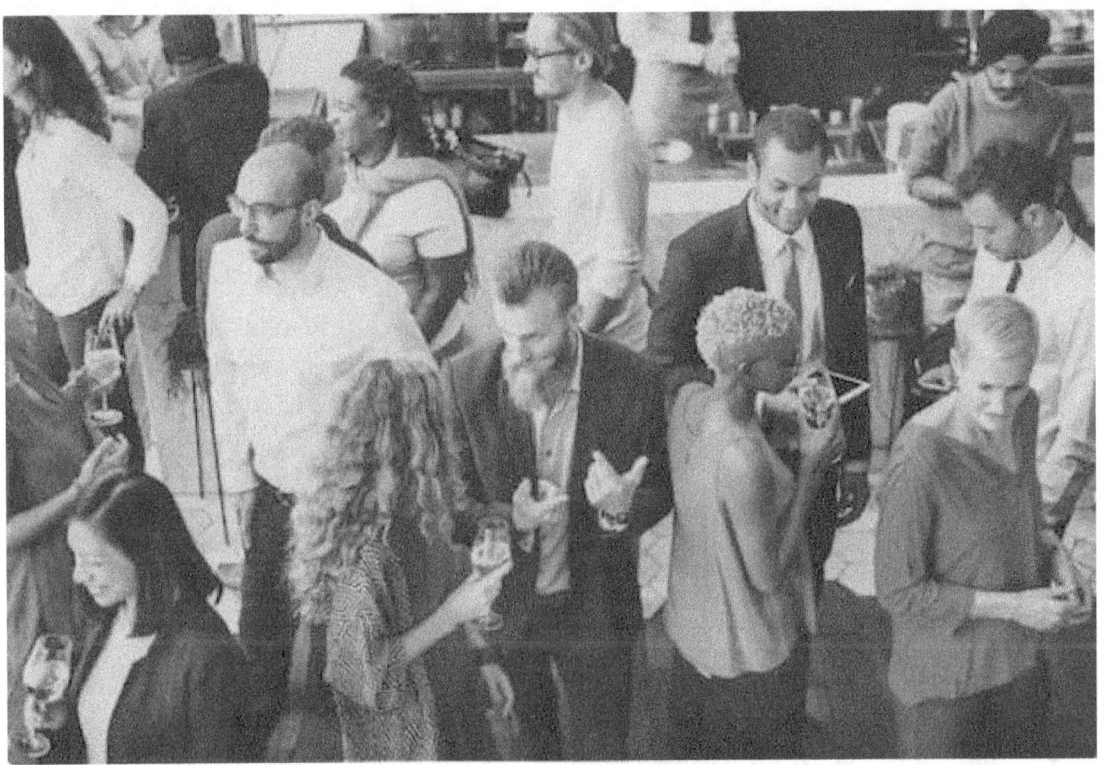

Yet many team meetings are fraught with inefficient communication dynamics. Perhaps one member of the team dominates the conversation, or someone else disengages and never participates, or someone discards the discussion.

Reflect on Current Dynamics

If you are a team leader, you may be able to make decisions that can change the dynamics of your team. If you're a team member, the more you know about healthy communication, the more you can argue for a change. The first move is to focus on the communication patterns of your team. Here are six questions to direct this reflection:

- What do I think about the interactions we've had in our team? What kind of dynamic do I see present?
- How do I feel about the conversations we've got right now?
- What do I want to make our team's discussions look and sound like?
- What are the meanings our discussions ought to have?
- How do I feel about conversations?

- What describes a good conversation for me, huh?

Identify the Outcome

Teams will take a big step towards better communication by identifying what they want to hear and see in group meetings and what they don't want to hear and see. When a team I worked with was in a particularly stormy process, participants made a list of what they needed to see and hear in group conversations. They included the following:

- Active listening by paraphrasing and answering follow-up, clarifying questions.
- Active listening by non-verbal communication (eye contact, nodding).
- Questions are grounded in a genuine investigation.
- Summary of each other's ideas.
- Invitations to the more silent participants.
- Make sure everyone's voice is heard.
- We are probing questions that are below the surface comments.
- A constructive clash of ideas.
- We are offering ideas, suggestions, strategies and next steps.
- Empathy for each other and others outside the team (including students, parents and managers).

They also listed what they didn't want to see and hear, which included:

- We are moving out of the subject and into lengthy digressions.
- She was dominating the conversation by talking too much or attempting to control the conversation.
- Being cynical.
- Disengagement and not involvement.
- Dismissing the thoughts of others with "yes, buts."
- Gossip about the others.
- You are blaming the wrong ones.
- To be distracted by other items (technology) or people.

Off to a Good Start

They discussed their responses at the start of each meeting, and each participant chose some of the positive attributes that it would concentrate on demonstrating. Sometimes the team asked the process observer to monitor what they had observed in terms of their contact and which of the elements they had shown.

After several months of close attention to their interactions by the use of this tool, this team's discussions improved dramatically.

Knowledge about how the team interacts and how you would like it to interact is a critical first step in changing dynamics. Without this contemplation, and without knowing the course you're trying to take, you won't be able to find a strategic path.

CHANGE YOUR MIND

Some people can change their minds as quickly as they can change their clothes. Even when they're shopping for clothes, they choose one item to purchase, then swap it for another, and they end up buying something completely different. Or they're going back and forth about what to order in a restaurant. But where it really counts change their feelings about themselves and their lives they behave as though their minds are frozen in stone. They refuse to acknowledge that the thoughts in their minds can only be views, not facts.

Thoughts have no control over us apart from the influence we bestow upon them. They are merely brief mental experiences that move through our heads, making room for the next. But when they're trapped in our minds and left to talk around unexamined, they can lead to persistent negative emotions such as anxiety, anger, and depression. Change your mind, change your mood. But how are you going to change your mind about your own thoughts? It begins by becoming mindful of your thoughts and relating them to your daily experiences. Schedule time with yourself at the end of the day to reflect on the events of the day by asking yourself questions like the following:

- What happened to me today that was upsetting?

- Did anyone say something that made me feel frustrated or depressed?

- Was there something unforeseen that changed my mood?
- What went wrong today, huh?

Follow up by asking yourself:
- What was going on in my mind at the time?
- What did I think or say to myself under my breath?
- What were the thoughts floating around in my head?
- Whose speech or whose words do they sound like?

Once you get used to analyzing your thoughts on a daily basis, try to catch them as they happen during the day, as discussed below.

When Is a Cause Not a Cause?

Each of us is a personal scientist, trying to figure out the causes of the events that happen in our daily lives. It is reasonable to see a cause-and-effect connection between events that happen contiguously — that is, linked in time and space.

Let's say something happens to you, and you'll soon begin to feel (emotional response). You may make the logical assumption that contiguity is equivalent to causality so that if one event follows another in time and space (daily interactions are accompanied by emotional reactions), it must be causally linked. Ipso facto, events (A) arise, and emotional reactions (B) result, so A must be the cause of B. This method of reasoning is based on a faulty premise that emotional reactions are the direct result of life's experiences. But (and this is a major but), we sometimes miss the intermediate step that links events with emotions. These missing links in the chain are private mental interactions that we call feelings.

Consider the causal relationship between the light switch flickering and the lights switching on. These two events are connected together so consistently in time and place that it is reasonable to assume that the flipping of the switch triggers the observed effect (the lights on). Yet one day, you happen to be flicking the switch, and nothing happens. Maybe the light is blown, or maybe the wiring is short. In a similar way, life events may seem to be a direct cause of emotional reactions, as B consistently follows A, but a complete picture of the cause needs to be taken into account on the surface of the mind, specifically the thoughts that intercede between life experiences and emotional reactions.

The proof is that two people may experience the same event but have very different emotional reactions. Or you may have experienced the same event yourself on separate occasions, but you had very different emotional reactions based on how you thought about each event at the time. Same case, different kind of results. I'm expecting you to think of examples from your own life of how different people were influenced by the same incident in different ways.

Key Steps to Changing Your Mind

Thoughts that seem to pop into our mind are called automatic thoughts. When negative automatic thoughts revive unchallenged in our brains, they can trigger a range of negative emotions.

Change your mind, change your mood, but how? It begins by catching disturbing thoughts, bringing them to the light of reality, and then substituting more logical ways of thinking by practicing what I call rational back-talk. Let's call this three-step SRS method: Pause, Reconsider and Substitute.

STEP 1: STOP

Trying to catch a thought is like holding water in your mouth. It seems to fall through it. To become a thought catcher, get used to checking what's on your mind anytime you feel frustrated, right then and there—using your thoughts as a reference to the substance of your mind.

People are typically more aware of what they feel (anger or fear is difficult to suppress, and with good reason) than they are conscious. Ask yourself, what's going on in my mind? What was I thinking about? What thoughts are related to the way I feel?

Stop whatever you do and put down some disturbing thoughts or ideas in your journal or notebook. In time, sort through your series of troubling thoughts. Do they fall into predictable patterns, such as the feelings you put themselves in, expect something bad to happen, exaggerate the effects of negative events, expect the worst, concentrate only on the negative, ignore the positive, blame yourself for other people's problems, and so on. Find the pattern that suits the way you think negatively. Or visit a cognitive behavioral therapist to help guide you through the process of recognizing the reasons for your personal thinking.

STEP 2: RETHINK

Analyze your thinking. Does that make sense, or is it twisted or exaggerated? Am I going to judge myself too harshly, more harshly than I would judge anyone else in the same situation? Weigh the evidence supporting the logic of the argument, and the evidence weighed against it. Consider the thinking to see if it's going to hold up under scrutiny. Tell yourself, who says it has to be like that? Whose speech or whose words do I sound like when I put myself down? And maybe most importantly, ask yourself whether the thinking is working for you (helping you move forward in your life) or against you (keeping you stuck and feeling miserable). Recognize that no one can make you feel mad (or any other emotion) without your permission. So maybe you're just not giving your permission this time.

STEP 3: SUBSTITUTE

When you recognize and question a troubling idea, change your mind by substituting logical alternative thinking in its place. To get started, let me offer a few examples from my patients of thinking replacement, or what I call logical back-talk, which they used to combat self-examination and self-judgement.

Take back your anger by responding back to your own angry thoughts and self-statements, as in the following examples:

Angering Self-Statements

- He's a cruel, cruel, disgusting guy to do what he did to me.
- I can't bear being treated like this, and I'm not going to take it.
- People are meant to be disciplined for stuff like this.
- I feel so bad about myself that I let this happen to me.
- No one has ever had to put up with something like this.
- No one should be allowed to treat me like that.
- I just can't walk away from it as nothing has happened.
- If I let him get away with this, he'll think I'm a wimp.

Rational Back-Talk to these Angering Self-Statements

1. What he did to me was thoughtless, but I'm not supposed to judge him on the basis of one encounter. How am I supposed to know what he's going through?
2. You've been through even worse than this. Calm down, man. Don't blow it out of proportion.
3. It's not up to me to determine who's to be disciplined. I wouldn't want any other people to judge me in general.
4. Don't say you're at fault immediately. Avoid dumping on your own.
5. How do you know what the people had to put up with? Anyway, what kind of difference does it make to me what other people have had to put up with?
6. Don't expect someone always to be aware of your best interests. He was behaving on the basis of his own best interests, not mine. It's just human.
7. You may, of course. When did indignation solve anything?
8. You don't have anything to say. If you let him control your acts, you're going to be reduced to his level.

OVERCOME YOUR DARK SIDE

Remember that time you were trying to act rationally, but something took over you, and you just couldn't help yourself? When you insulted your wife, lost your temper at work, or broke your diet, and went on a binge to eat? This is your 'other side' (also called 'shadow') talking.

Your shadow is the deep and dark place inside your own mind. The place of your past's fears, issues, and repressed experiences. The one that you refuse to believe still exists. But once you embrace it, it's going to try to take over.
So, in this part, we're going to talk about your shadow. And how you can't let it get in your way.

What Does Your Dark Side Really Mean?

Here's what the dark side (also known as 'The Shadow Self') means, according to Carl Jung, one of the most influential psychologists and psychoanalysts of all time:
"The Shadow Self is an abstraction that is part of the unconscious mind and is composed of repressed thoughts, instincts, urges, vulnerabilities, desires, perversions and disturbing fears."
In other words, your shadow is that dark part of yourself that you just don't want to believe exists... but that still takes over in particularly stressful or tough times.

What Are You Supposed to Do with Your Dark Side?

As counter-intuitive as it might be, through suppressing your emotions, desires, and fears, you are constructing a false image that you are projecting to the world, which is not truly yours. You build a 'better' version of yourself that you just can't keep up with. And, at the end of the day, you are human — just like everyone else.

We live in a time when people are placing 50 filters on their selfies to make themselves look fine. 'The guy' is the face you show to the world, your ideal self, and the way you want to be viewed by other people.

If you concentrate on feeding the 'best' part of you, you're bound to fail. This is going to happen because you can't grow only the 'presentable' part of yourself, you have to consider all sides of the coin. But how are you going to do that, exactly?

How Can You Accept Your Dark Side?

Knowing yourself is the best way to achieve prosperity, happiness and harmony in your lives. By accepting the dark parts of yourself, you open the door to your deepest fears and traumatic memories in a way that sets them — and you — free from repression. This is a really rough patch, and it's not a good idea to walk alone, so I strongly encourage you to seek professional support.

The only way to self-love is to embrace your shadow. You can't enjoy the pieces of yourself that you deem attractive and ignore those that you don't want to identify with. Realize that you need to understand and embrace every aspect of your personality and appearance.

One of the things I recommend to my clients is to take a good look at themselves in the mirror. Not to criticize, not to try to change something. Only look at the person who looks at them right in the eye. This person is the most important and most powerful person in the world since he is the one who creates his entire existence.

Another strategy is to list all the stuff you don't like about your personality and try to reframe them in a positive way. It's all about the outlook. Let me give you an example: "I hate myself for quickly getting angry and screaming about stupid things" can become "I'm temperamental and sensitive, and sometimes I get easily irritated. I support myself, and I love myself as I am."

There are a lot of ways you can embrace the dark side. We are all different from each other, and, sadly, there is no simple solution to alter the way you see yourself. Some people spend years on counselling or coaching, and others get results for 1-2 months. It depends on past wounds, the degree of the open-mindedness of the client and the determination of the client to achieve the desired outcome.

How do you confront your dark side?

The remedy to face the dark side of your mind is to practice it consciously. There are things that can't be avoided, but you should be faced with those that can, and you should be acquainted with them. The greatest challenge is to immerse yourself in your mind and illuminate all that is concealed within it.
The dark side hides much more than unfulfilled desires, thwarted hopes, or broken dreams, but you alone can delve into it and explore.
Any time the depression comes up in your life, any time you feel like something evil is trying to take over you, that's when you have to try to find out why, without feeling any guilt.
You have to recognize that there is a dark side to your mind that is there and that it won't go away just because you want to repress it. Repression is only going to make it bigger, and with more power, it will erupt as soon as it has a chance.
Be brave, guy. Be frank with yourself and strive to free yourself from this negativity. Meditation can help you do that. Coaching can be helpful, too. Even though art, you can take the worst things that are locked in your mind, channeling the negativity.
Only by doing what is concealed from your dark side will you be able to regain control of your life and learn to manage negativity so that it does not influence you.

How to Know When you've Made It

One of the easiest ways to tell if you're going to get there is to take a hard and honest look at the emotions you feel every day. If you have negative feelings and are conscious of what triggered them, it's safe to say that you're aware of your dark side and don't try to hide it anymore. Another indication of this is that you don't slip into old negative habits that often, and even if you do, you know exactly how to get out of them in a shorter time than before. Each and every one of us is different, and the results can vary. However, there is one thing in common: when you embrace the dark side, you feel better about yourself, your self-confidence is strengthened, and you shift your perspective of life. The moment you understand that life is neither good nor bad is the moment you start taking responsibility for your own actions and accepting yourself.

MANIPULATION

Manipulation is a common phenomenon, present in almost every area of our social life. It is a puzzling motivating activity aimed at intervening with another person's decision-making process, usually without his or her permission. This kind of interference happens indirectly through the use of morally dubious techniques such as coercion, diversion, and misdirection.

The trickery associated with coercion allows the practice to appear in almost limitless variations and under several different guises, from a strong tool in the service of indecent propaganda to altruistic methods in psychotherapy and education. Indeed, social scientists have found out that a successful improvement in human decision-making and actions cannot be accomplished without a certain degree of coercion.

Manipulation is not coercion; it is not simply deceit. This enigmatic phenomenon is situated somewhere in the grey region between these motivating behaviors, and this grey spot poses significant difficulties in characterizing manipulation and assessing its effect. The qualified manipulator shall pursue tactics in such a way as to obscure the moral and legal analysis of his acts. His complex and illusory strategies of manipulation question the orthodoxy of the leading advocates of an open society. The problem exists in almost every field that one can imagine, from politics to advertising to education and even to the most intimate relationships.

For example, where is the boundary between sexual assault and legal courtship? How is it possible to differentiate between respectable and indecent propaganda? What exactly is the distinction between fair and unreasonable market influence? How can people be drawn to new ideas because they are not inclined to pay attention? How do the social reformer, the artist, and the pioneer question traditional thinking and open new perspectives? What is the most successful way to open a national discussion on critical, important topics that almost everybody in society considers to be taboos?

Exploring the problem from this point of view is helpful in developing a better understanding of the unique characteristics of deception and helps us to avoid answering tricky questions that cannot be answered in a satisfactory manner.

Mental Health Effects Of Manipulation

If they are not handled, exploitation may lead to poor mental health outcomes for those who are exploited. Chronic coercion in close relationships may also be a sign of emotional violence, which in some situations may have a similar effect on trauma — especially when the victim of manipulation is made to feel guilty or ashamed.

Victims of chronic manipulation may:

- Feel down.

- Being an agony.

- Develop unhealthful coping habits.

- Always try to please the manipulative guy.

- Lie about their emotions.

- Put the needs of another person above their own needs.

- Find it hard to trust someone.

In some cases, deception may be so common that it leads the victim to doubt their perception of reality. Gaslight's classic film depicted one of those stories in which a woman's husband secretly exploited her until she no longer trusted her own perceptions. For example, the husband secretly turned down the gas lights and convinced his wife that the dim light was all in her head.

MANIPULATION IN RELATIONSHIPS

Long-term exploitation can have significant consequences in close relationships, including those between friends, family members, and romantic partners. Manipulation can harm the relationship and lead to the poor mental health of those involved.

In a marriage or partnership, coercion can cause a partner to feel bullied, alienated, or worthless. Even in healthy relationships, one partner can unwittingly manipulate the other to avoid confrontation or even to prevent them from feeling burdened. Many people may even realize that they are being exploited in their relationship and choose to neglect or downplay it. Manipulating intimate relationships can take many forms, including exaggeration, remorse, gift-giving, or selective affection, deception, and passive aggression.

Parents who abuse their children can set their children up for shame, depression, anxiety, eating disorders, and other mental health conditions. One study also found that parents who frequently use manipulation tactics on their children can increase the likelihood that their children will also use manipulative behavior. Signs of coercion in the parent-child relationship may include making the child feel guilty, a lack of accountability on the part of the parent, a downplaying of the child's successes, and a need to be involved in many aspects of the child's life.

People may also feel exploited if they are part of partnerships that have become toxic. In manipulative friendships, one person may use others to meet his or her own needs at the expense of his or her friend. A manipulative friend may use guilt or manipulation to gain favors, such as borrowing money, or they may only reach out to that friend when they need to fulfil their own emotional needs, and they may find excuses when their friend needs them.

EXAMPLES OF MANIPULATIVE BEHAVIOR

Sometimes, people may manipulate others unconsciously, without being fully aware of what they're doing, while others may actively work on strengthening their manipulation tactics. Some signs of manipulation include:

- Passive-aggressive behavior.
- Implicit threats to you.
- Dishonesty.
- The withholding of information.
- I am isolating a person from a loved one.
- The lighting of petrol.
- Abuse of verbs.
- Use sex to achieve goals.

Since the motivations behind the manipulation can vary from unconscious to malicious, it is important to identify the circumstances of the manipulation that is taking place. Although cutting things off can be crucial in situations of abuse, a therapist may help people learn how to cope with or challenge others' manipulative behavior.

How To Spot Manipulation

We all want to meet our needs, but manipulators use underhanded methods. Manipulation is a way to manipulate someone with indirect, misleading or abusive techniques covertly. Manipulation may seem innocent, or even pleasant, or flattering as if the individual has the greatest concern in mind, but in fact, it is intended to achieve an ulterior motive. Other times, its veiled aggression, and when coercive tactics are used, the goal is simply gaining power. You may not know that you are unintentionally threatened.

When you grew up being abused, it's harder to see what's going on, because it feels familiar. You may have an internal feeling of discomfort or rage, but on the surface, the manipulator may use terms that are flattering, gratifying, rational, or play on your guilt or compassion, so you override your instincts and don't know what to say. Codependents have difficulty being direct and assertive, and they may use coercion to get their way. They are also easy prey to being exploited by narcissists, sociopaths, and other co-dependents, like abusers.

Manipulative Tactics

Favorite tools of the manipulators are guilt, complaining, comparing, lying, denying (including explanations and rationalizations), feigning ignorance, or innocence ('Who Me!?' defense), blame, bribery, undermining, mind games, assumptions, 'foot-in-the-door' reversals, emotional blackmail, evasiveness, forgetfulness, false concern, sympathy, apology, flattery, and gifts and favors. Manipulators often use remorse by saying, explicitly or through the inference, "After all I have done or achieved," or by constantly acting vulnerable and powerless. They could equate you negatively to someone else or mobilize hypothetical supporters to their cause, saying, "Everyone" or "Even so and so thinks XYZ," or "says XYZ about you."

Some manipulators reject commitments, deals, or discussions, or start an argument, and accuse you of something you haven't done to gain sympathy and control. This method may be used to break a deadline, commitment or agreement. Parents regularly exploit bribery-everything from, "Finish your dinner to get dessert," to, "No video games before your homework is done." I was bribed by the offer of a car that I needed to travel to summer school, on the condition that I choose to go to the college that my parents had chosen rather than the one that I had preferred. I've really regretted taking the bribe. When you do that, it destroys your self-respect.

Manipulators sometimes make assumptions about your motives or convictions, and then respond to them as if they were real to justify their feelings or actions while denying what you say in conversation. They could behave as if something had been agreed upon or decided when it had not been decided to ignore any criticism or concern that you might have raised.

The "foot-in-the-door" technique is a tiny request that you agree to make, followed by a real request. It's harder to say no because you said yes. The reversal turns the words around to mean something you didn't intend to do. When you object, the manipulators turn the tables on you to make the injured party. Now it's all about them and their grievances, and you're on the defensive. The fake concern is sometimes used to undermine your decisions and confidence in the form of warnings or to worry about you.

Emotional Blackmail

Emotional blackmail is an emotional tactic that may include the use of anger, intimidation, threats, embarrassment or guilt. Shaming you is a way to create self-doubt and make you feel vulnerable. It can even be said in a compliment: "I'm surprised that all of you will stoop to that!" A classic trick is to threaten you with threats, indignation, allegations, or dire warnings, such as, "At your age, you'll never find anyone else if you quit," or to play the victim: "I'll die without you."

Blackmailers will threaten you with rage, too, so you're going to sacrifice your needs and wants. If that doesn't work, they suddenly switch to a lighter mood. You're so happy that you're willing to accept whatever you're looking for. They could bring up something that you feel guilty or ashamed of from the past to threaten or intimidate you, such as, "I'll tell the XYZ children if you do XYZ."

Victims of extortionists who have certain personality disorders, such as borderline or narcissistic PD, are likely to experience a psychological FOG that stands for Anxiety, Obligation, and Guilt, an acronym developed by Susan Forward. The victim feels afraid to cross the manipulator, feels obliged to comply with his or her order, and feels too guilty not to do so. The shame and guilt can be used specifically on charges that you are "selfish" (the worst sin to many co-dependents) or that "you just think about yourself," "you don't care about me," or that "you've got it so convenient."

Codependency

Codependents have rarely been assertive. They might say whatever they think someone wants to hear to get along or be loved, but later they do what they want. This is also passive-aggressive behavior. Rather than answer a question that could lead to a confrontation, they are evasive, change the subject, or use blame and denial (including explanations and rationalizations) to avoid being incorrect. Because they find it so hard to say no, they may say yes, followed by complaints about how difficult it is to accommodate the request. When confronted, because of their profound shame, the co-dependents have difficulty accepting responsibility, so they deny it and blame others or make empty excuses to keep the peace.

They make use of charm and flattery and give favors, support and gifts to be accepted and cherished. Criticism, guilt, and self-pity are also used to manipulate what they want: "Why do you just think of yourself and never ask or help me with my problems? I helped you." Acting as a victim is a way to manipulate guilt. Addicts regularly deny, lie, and exploit to maintain their addictions. Their partners often exploit, for example, by covering or diluting a drug or alcohol abuser or by other deceptive behavior. They may also lie or tell half-truths in order to avoid confrontation or control the behavior of the addict.

Passive-aggression

Passive-aggressive behavior may also be used to exploit. If you're having trouble saying no, you may consent to something you don't want, and then get your way by failing, being late, or doing it half-heartedly. Usually, passive aggression is a way of expressing anger. Failing "on purpose" is easily ignoring something you don't want to do and getting back to your partner-like forgetting to pick up your spouse's clothes from the cleaners. Sometimes this is done unconsciously, but it's still a way to express rage.

How To Deal With Manipulative People

When coercion becomes harmful, coping with the actions of others may be exhausting. Workplace coercion has been shown to reduce performance, and the deceptive actions of loved ones may make the truth seem questionable. If you feel that you are being abused in any kind of relationship, it might be helpful to:

Unsubscribe. If someone is trying to get a specific emotional response from you, choose not to send it to them. For e.g., if a deceptive friend is known to flatter you before asking for an implicit favor, don't play along — rather, respond politely, and move the conversation along.

Be sure about that. Often deception can involve attempts by one person to cause another person to question their ability, instincts, or even truth. If this happens, it might help to stick to your story; however, if this happens regularly in a close relationship, it may be time to leave.

Pick out the manipulative actions as they happen. Maintaining your mind on how the actions of the other person impact you rather than beginning with an accusatory comment may also help you reach a resolution, thus stressing that their coercive methods will not work on you.

Stay on the subject. When you point out a behavior that makes you feel abused, the other person can try to mitigate the situation or complicate the situation by raising other issues as a diversion. Remember your main point and stick to it.

Addressing Manipulation In Therapy

Treatment and therapy for manipulative behavior can depend to a large extent on the underlying behavioral problems. For example, if coercion is caused by an underlying mental health issue, individual therapy may help the person to understand why their conduct is unhealthful for themselves and those around them. A psychologist may also be able to help the deceptive person learn the ability to interact with others while recognizing their weaknesses and addressing the underlying insecurities that may lead to their behavior.

Many mental health issues, such as borderline personality, can cause people to feel insecure in relationships, causing them to deceive in order to feel secure. In such situations, a therapist may help a person to resolve their mental health problems, which, in turn, may reduce their anxiety and help them feel comfortable in their relationships.

SOCIAL INTELLIGENCE AT WORK

Social intelligence is the ability to connect and to establish relationships with empathy and assertiveness. It comes from self-awareness and the practice of proper emotional control. We may assume it's closely related to emotional intelligence, but it's not exactly the same thing.

Emotional intelligence arises from introspection and encompasses topics such as emotional perception and the role of emotions in the problem-solving process. It has something to do with how people handle themselves before they get in touch with another human.

When you start communicating, social intelligence skills should be activated, along with emotional intelligence, which involves activities such as speech, conversation, listening, conciliation, and learning by contact with others.

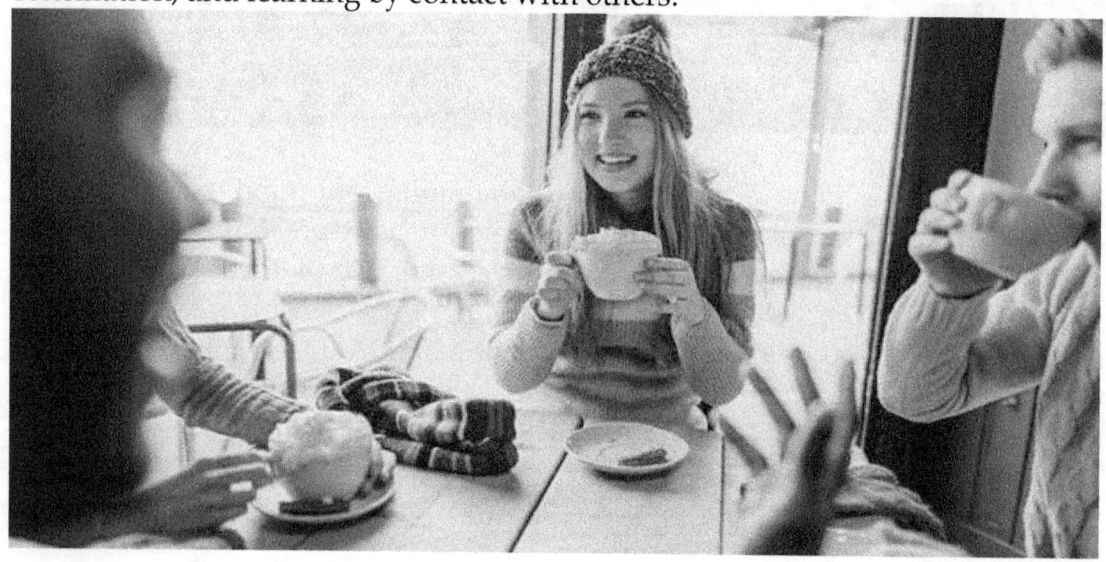

Everybody deserves to feel loved and content both at home and at work. The secret is a good relationship. Research has indicated that social intelligence, such as SQ, is important for successful leadership and to help teams work well together.

Social Intelligence (SQ) is closely related and specifically connected to Emotional Intelligence (EQ). In fact, psychologists became aware of our Intellectual Capacity (IQ), which included things like our rational thinking and analytical skills as well as our memory to store different types of knowledge.

Psychologists then further developed and studied this idea and explored EQ, which focuses on topics such as self-esteem, self-assessment, self-confidence, self-motivation, social knowledge, etc. Essentially, factors that affect emotions like self-control, trustworthiness, adaptability, self-driving, and dedication and, of course, social skills, to name a few.

Reasons why social intelligence matters at work

Reason 1

The willingness to get along with your colleagues is going to get you their support. But that's a lot more than the previous argument. It's the commitment you need to make in establishing stronger working relationships so that people want to work with you. If not, no one will work for the same target, and no one will be able to work effectively as a team.

Reason 2

You need to consider the influence your actions have on other employees. Think of the idea that we were taught as children to "do to someone what you would like them to do to you." If someone feels important to the team, he or she will contribute the value you need. It also helps to align each team member with the team's goals.

Reason 3

In a culturally diverse workforce within South African companies, people feel different and react differently to circumstances based on their cultural differences, experiences and backgrounds. Social interactions, such as culture days or cultural exchanges, help a lot to overcome these differences in understanding why people are acting in a certain way in certain circumstances. Communication skills should be developed and adapted to reflect these cultural differences. Respectfor each other grows in such a way.

Reason 4

Social-emotional contact will also help to keep you at work and to be a sought-after future employee. There are many managers who claim that because of a lack of social intelligence, people have lost their jobs or have never been considered for promotion. Why? And we need people to be able to work together to achieve a common purpose, which is what the workforce is. The workforce needs team members, and solo acts will not support the company's growth and the creation of its employees.

When you speak to the team leaders, the manager or project manager and the coordinators, you quickly find out that their main challenge is 'staff issues,' which are getting the team members to work together. In order to benefit from social intelligence, we need to learn the skills to interpret non-verbal actions in order to understand other people's feelings better, so that we can better connect to each other. This is not something you are born with, but a particular skill set you need to learn and improve on.

What Abilities Does Social Intelligence Convey?

Social intelligence integrates the skills needed for successful communication based on empathy, self-knowledge, listening and reading of emotions. These skills are as follows:

1. Verbal and non-verbal fluency

Conversation skills are the most fundamental form of social intelligence. Verbal and non-verbal gestures are the main channels for transmitting messages. The first step towards effective communication is the use of the right words, the ideal tone and having clear intention.

2. Knowledge of social rules and roles

Knowing their social norms, traditions, and idiosyncrasies is a fundamental skill for socially intelligent people when you communicate with a group. This promotes contact with individuals belonging to various social classes, such as people of different ages, cultures, religions or cultural identities.

3. Listening skills

Active listening is essential to the growth of social intelligence. It helps to communicate with others, avoids conflict, and encourages learning through dialogue. This makes a significant contribution to personal growth.

4. Understanding how other people's emotions work

Understanding what activates people's feelings (either negatively or positively) is a core component of the practice of empathy. This expertise allows communication that takes into account other people's strengths and sensitivities, making the message genuine and effective.

5. Playing social roles efficiently

This capacity helps people to adjust to various social situations. Having a good understanding of what is required of us in a number of different situations decreases tension in every situation and makes for more positive interactions.

6. Self-Image and impression management

This is the ability to express ourselves in a way that interacts with others without pulling too far away from our natural personality. The goal is to maintain a positive attitude that appeals to others, show compassion and strengthen our sense of self.

Why Is Social Intelligence Necessary For Education And Future Jobs?

Social intelligence uses the management of emotions and self-awareness to enhance relationships, promote leadership and facilitate the performance of specific intellectual tasks.

There has been a lot of discussion about automation and the possible unemployment it could bring. The capacity of workers to re-skill, adapt and improve continuously would be essential for them to retain their position in the labor market.

The less sensitive a job is to computerization, the more important it will be to humans. The political analyst and comedian John Oliver gives a sharp insight into this subject. In an automation article, he offers a detailed perspective on why social intelligence is so crucial to creating jobs that only humans can do: "You can do a variety of non-routine tasks that involve social intelligence, nuanced critical thinking, and imaginative problem-solving," Oliver said in response to a boy who asked about potential jobs that robots could not do in the future.

Social intelligence is necessary to activate the skills of effective communication, conversation and collaboration to build an efficient and productive working environment. Until recently, social intelligence was a concern that only few people had, mainly because they already had the right way of thinking and learned the related skills along the way, but training to improve social intelligence is relatively new.

Today, teaching social intelligence is invaluable because it is the best opportunity to create and sustain a healthy working culture and to preserve employment in an age of increasing automation. Students need opportunities to cultivate social intelligence, starting at the first level of schooling, so that they can learn it through their school years and master it in their adult lives.

HOW TO STOP PROCRASTINATION

Procrastination is not just a human problem. Newton's First Rule of Motion states that the body will remain at rest until it has been pushed to do otherwise. Dare we say that? The whole world is procrastinating.

But that doesn't mean it's a smart idea just because procrastination is universal. And so often, we find ourselves procrastinating when we know we're not supposed to. We're muttering, "I really ought to be working," as we stalk our sophomore year homecoming date on Facebook, stand in front of the open fridge for the fourth time in an hour, or remember we're watching banjo lessons on YouTube because we don't own a banjo.

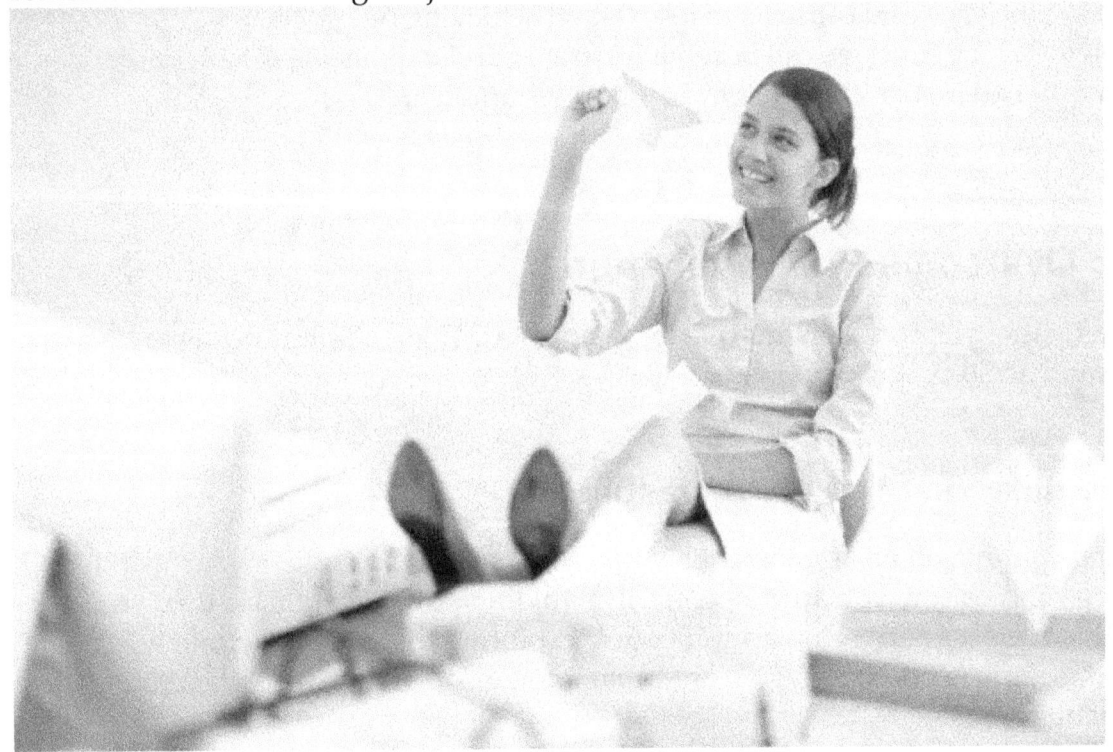

Procrastination can also go beyond work, influencing other vital parts of our lives and not having this annoying symptom tested leaves an unknown condition untreated. Avoiding a tough discussion will only intensify the dispute. And delaying a significant life decision, such as breaking up, making a serious commitment, going back to school, or eventually changing career paths, can lead to years of running.

Is Procrastination the Same as Being Lazy?

Procrastination is often associated with laziness, but it is quite distinct.
Procrastination is an aggressive method – you want to do something else instead of the job you know you should do. Laziness, on the other hand, indicates apathy, inactivity, and inability to act.
Procrastination typically means avoiding an unpleasant but potentially more important task, in favor of one that is more fun or simpler.
But giving in to this instinct may have severe consequences. For example, even mild episodes of procrastination can make us feel guilty or ashamed of ourselves. It can lead to a decrease in efficiency and cause us to lose out on achieving our goals.
If we go on for a long time, we can become frustrated and disillusioned with our jobs, which can lead to dissatisfaction and even job losses, in severe cases.

How To Overcome Procrastination

As for other patterns, procrastination can be conquered. Take the steps below to help you cope with and avoid procrastination:

Recognize That You're Procrastinating

You could be putting off an assignment because you had to re-prioritize your workload. If for a very good reason, you are momentarily avoiding a significant task, then you are not actually procrastinating. However, if you start putting things off indefinitely, or changing the emphasis because you want to stop doing something, then you are procrastinating.
You may also be procrastinating if you:

- Round out your day with low-priority jobs.

- Leave an item on your To-Do list for a long time, even though it's significant.

- Read emails a few times without making a decision about what to do with them.

- Start a high-priority job and then get off to make a coffee.

- Fill your time with the unimportant things that other people are asking you to do, instead of moving on with the important tasks that are already on your list.

- Wait for the "right moment" or wait for the "right time" to get to grips with the mission.

Work Out WHY you're Procrastinating

You need to understand why you're going to procrastinate before you can start tackling it.

For example, are you avoiding a specific task because you find it tedious or unpleasant? If so, take action to get it out of the way quickly, so that you can concentrate on the aspects of your work that you find more enjoyable.

Poor organization can lead to procrastination. Organized people have successfully solved this because they use prioritized To-Do lists to create effective schedules. These tools allow you to organize your tasks by priority and time.

Even if you're coordinated, you can always feel frustrated by a mission. You may have concerns about your abilities and worry about failing, so you put it off and seek comfort in doing work that you know you're capable of achieving.

Some people fear success as much as they fear failure. They conclude that progress would lead them to be swamped with demands to take on more tasks.

Ironically, perfectionists prefer to be procrastinators. Sometimes, they prefer to avoid doing a job that they don't believe they have the skills to do, rather than doing it imperfectly.

Bad decision-making is another significant cause of procrastination. If you can't decide what to do, you're likely to postpone taking action if you do the wrong thing.

Warning:

For certain people, procrastination is more than a bad habit; it is a symptom of a significant underlying health problem. For example, procrastination is associated with ADHD, OCD, anxiety, and depression.

Research also shows that procrastination can be a source of severe stress and illness. So, if you suffer from persistent or crippling procrastination, one of these disorders might be to blame, and you should seek advice from a qualified professional.

Adopt Anti-Procrastination Strategies

Procrastination is the result of a profoundly rooted pattern of actions. This means you probably won't be able to crack it overnight. Habits begin being habits when you start doing them, so use as many of the techniques below as possible to give yourself the best chance of success.

- Forgive yourself that you have procrastinated in the past. Studies show that self-forgiveness will make you feel more optimistic about yourself and reduce the probability of procrastination in the future.

- Come on to the job. Concentrate on doing this, not avoiding it. Write down the tasks you need to do, and determine the time to complete them. This will allow you to take a positive approach to your job.

- Promise yourself a reward for that. If you're completing a challenging task in time, reward yourself with a treat, such as a slice of cake or a coffee from your favorite coffee shop. And make sure you remember how good it feels to finish things off!

- Tell someone to help you out. Peer Pressure is working! That's the idea behind self-help programs. If you don't have someone to ask, an online tool like Procraster will help you control yourself.

- Act as you're going to do things. Tackle activities as soon as they emerge, rather than allowing them to pile up for another day.

- Rephrase the internal conversation. For example, the phrases "need to" and "have to" mean that you don't have a choice in what you do. This can make you feel helpless and even lead to self-sabotage. However, saying, "I want to" means that you own a project and can make you feel more in control of your workload.

- Minimize the distractions. Switch off your email and social media, and stop sitting anywhere near a TV while you're working!

- The aim is to "eat the elephant beetle" first thing, every day! Get those things you find the least fun out of the way early. This will give you the rest of the day to concentrate on the work you find more enjoyable.

Tip:
An alternative solution is to embrace the "art of delay." Research suggests that "productive procrastination" – that is, intentionally avoiding getting started so that you can concentrate on other pressing tasks – will make you feel more inspired and driven to get things done. This strategy will work especially well if you're someone who thrives under pressure.
However, if you plan to procrastinate deliberately, be sure to avoid placing your co-workers under any needless, uncomfortable or unwanted strain!

CURE YOUR RELATIONSHIP

Relationships often go south. Humans are complicated beings, and our love life is even more complicated. As the days go by and our lives get busier, it is often our relationship with our loved ones that struggle the most. As communication and relationship break down, it takes to know both yourself and your partner to make the substantive adjustments required to turn things around.

Like so many things, it can be difficult to focus on our intimate relationships. Often the complaints and disagreements that we have with our spouse run deep. It can be hard to forgive or to move on when there are feelings like remorse or guilt at play.

If you want to re-establish your relationship, you need to be ready for a fresh start, but that starts with a deeper understanding of your love and begins with embracing yourself. Broken items may be repaired, but repairing is sometimes more complicated than breaking. Are you ready to repair your relationship with you? Then get yourself together to repair it.

HEAR—To Hear Your Partner, Stay Present and Listen

When your partner talks, make an effort to remain emotionally present and listen. Open your heart and let your defenses down. It's not about defending yourself; it's about trying to understand your partner and learning to meet each other's needs.

Listen to her vocabulary to the non-verbal signals of feeling. Does she have an angry look in her face or sorrow in her eyes? Is his body language accessible and reaching out to you, or is it locked and guarded? What do you think your partner feels like? What are the needs that have not been met (such as affection, companionship, understanding, power, or respect)? The best way to soothe a frustrated partner is to let him know that you're hearing and respecting his needs — and willing to make adjustments to meet them better.

EMPATHIZE—Allow Your Partner's Experience to Deeply Affect You

When you think you understand what your partner is feeling and have checked with him, pay attention to what you feel when you see him feeling this way. It is particularly important to look below the surface for softer, more delicate feelings. My clients also show frustration because what lies underneath is feeling trapped, depressed, or lonely. Can you stay with your wife and get in contact with her deeper experience, maybe feel discomfort because she's in discomfort? Will you feel compassion and let him know that his display of pain or rage has a profound impact on you? Your first instinct to hear your partner's frustration may be to try to fix the problem or provide advice. Sometimes, though, this guidance tends to be dismissive or judgmental, which may make things worse. On the other hand, being emotionally involved and showing compassion can provide therapeutic comfort and connection. That's what your partner wants a lot of times.

ACT—Take Action to Address Concerns and Show Willingness to Change

The next step is to commit to deliberate action to meet the needs and interests of your partner. These acts can range from helping more with dishes, calling your wife during the day to let her know that you're thinking about her, to spending less money because it makes her nervous. When your wife knows that you take her needs seriously, she's more likely to feel appreciated and supported. This will lead to a positive cycle in which your partner appreciates you and feels more caring towards you. You don't have to be perfect — just the fact that you care and want to improve is enough to make most people feel respected.

LOVE—Feel and Express Unconditional Love

Make room in your life to consciously reconnect with your partner's romantic feelings, even though recent experiences have made you feel distant or frustrated. Think of the good qualities that initially attracted you to him. You may want to look at old pictures or imagine special times in your relationship, or the hopes and dreams you've had together. Will you find a way to forgive yourself and your partner for the mistakes you both made that got you off track? Would you like to reach out to him and show your love and affection verbally or by action, such as preparing a meal or writing a note? Love is described as a concern for the well-being of others and a warm feeling that you have towards others. Do not make your expressions of love dependent on what your partner does, but rather reach out and show unconditional compassion, encouragement, empathy, and forgiveness. If there are unanswered confidence issues that impede your willingness to love your partner openly, think about the next steps you might take to address these issues and what it will take to rebuild trust.

HOW TO INFLUENCE PEOPLE

Leadership is all about the power of individuals. When you have an effect on other people's lives and do something that makes them feel affected, that's how you affect other people.
You need to know the strategies to manipulate so that you can use them to your advantage.
It gives you a mindset of leadership that develops and makes you a great influencer.
If you want to change the lives of other people, you need to influence them, and this will make you a more compassionate and authoritative person.

Give them what they want.

If you want to influence people, you need to give people exactly what they want. And everyone wants what they want, not what you like.

Forget about you; think about it. When you think of other people and their needs, it's going to make you into a better person in their eyes.

They're going to love you when you give what they want. They are going to give you more respect and authority.

Most people worry about themselves. So, to manipulate others, start giving them what they want.

Make others feel important.

People are going to do something for you if you make others feel important. It's the most critical secret to influencing others.

They all want to feel important. You also want to feel significant.

Right?

It's exactly this. If you make them feel secure, they're more likely to stay in your possession.

You can't make anyone do what you want them to do if they want to do things on their own.

For example, if you ask the sweeper to clean the floors, he'll do it, but he's not going to like you.

But if you let him know that he's valuable because he's always helping you to make your office cleaner, he's going to do it with more zeal and enjoy your actions.

Connect with emotions.

When you interact with other people's feelings, they're more likely to do things for you. You don't need to ask them about that.

You need to bind your feelings to them to make them more intuitive. This will help you control others and give you the role of leader.

However, if you can link other people's emotions to a target, you can move your business to the next level.

They're going to do something to reach the target for you because your desires and feelings are related to the same goal.

Empower them.

When you inspire people, you gain more authority.
As they say, people will forget what you said, people will forget what you did, but they will never forget how you made them feel.
Start inspiring them, and you're going to be on the road to influencing others.
Successful people inspire their co-workers, which helps them to become a great influencer.

Respect other people's opinion.

Never ever say "you're wrong" to anyone. Respect the opinion of other people as well. They might believe in something different, and they think they're right from their viewpoint.
If they say something that isn't right to you, instead of saying "you're wrong." Say this "I respect your opinion, but it's different from my point of view."
Ask them, would you like to know why?
It's time to tell them what you think without hurting their self-esteem.
This is the best way to get to know a person if you want to influence people.

Show sympathy.

Suppose you see someone making a mistake. Never scold them. Bear in mind that they are still human beings.

People make a mistake, but it's your job to help them not repeat it again.

If you want to influence others, you need to tell them in a particular way that helps them to understand you better without getting hurt.

Yeah, how are you going to tell them?

Oh, look. Whenever someone makes a mistake, remind them that you made that mistake, too. This is going to create a sense of sympathy. People will understand you better when you do that.

Tell them, I've made the same mistake, but I've never done it twice, and I believe you're never going to do it again.

Which Influence Tactic Is Right For You?

Here's how to choose the best tactics to affect the situation. To understand what could work best for a specific task or plan, consider the following:

- Review the situation. Why are you interested in work? Why do you need the help of this person? What are the outcomes you're trying to achieve by manipulating this person? Be specific on who you intend to influence and what you want to do.

Ok, know your audience. Identify and appreciate the stakeholders. Both of them would have unique concerns and issues, as well as their own goals, viewpoints and objectives. Various groups and individuals may involve different approaches to influence. Tailor the impact plan for a single person — taking into account individual characteristics, goals and priorities — as well as organizational roles and responsibilities.

- Please check your performance. What techniques do you use most of the time? Which seems to be the most effective? What new strategies should you have used in this situation? Draw on others, too, for advice or coaching. For example, if you still rely on rational appeals, have a co-worker who is a good collaborator to help you think about your collaboration strategies and arguments.

- Brainstorm the solution to this. What kind of tactics would work best? How do you make an emotional or collective appeal? What exactly do you say and do to use any kind of tactics? Anticipate potential responses and plan your answer. What counter-arguments do you use?

At first, you might want to try new, one-on-one influence tactics in low-risk situations. Focus on improving the four main skills required to influence others. As you become more flexible and experienced, you can gain confidence in your ability to influence teams and larger groups and to convince others in higher-level situations.

But consider shifting strategy right away if you have an urgent problem that has stalled due to a lack of buy-in or funding. Will a more pragmatic, emotional, or collaborative approach make any difference? If so, go ahead and try to appeal from a different angle — you may find yourself more powerful than you've thought.

HOW TO ANALYZE PEOPLE

If by psychologically analyzing people, you mean using their words and behaviors to draw conclusions about how people think, I think this is something that almost all of us do when we communicate with someone else, and it's totally normal. However, the way you word your question makes me think that you assume that psychology is some sort of magic trick you can use to see into people's heads and control them. You don't need to be a psychologist to influence people, and getting a psychological understanding of how people want to behave doesn't inherently grant you the power to manipulate them. The main purpose of psychological research is to gain insight into the way people think, and why, in order to share this knowledge with individuals and society as a whole in order to change it.

Techniques in the Art of Reading People

The First Technique: Observe Body Language Cues

Research has shown that words account for just 7% of how we communicate, while our body language (55 per cent) and voice tone (30 per cent) account for the remainder. Here, surrendering to focus is letting go of working too hard to decipher body language signals. Don't get overly intense or overly analytical. Stay relaxed and in a fluid state. Be relaxed, sit back, and just enjoy.

1. Pay Attention to Appearance

When others dress, take notice: are they wearing a power suit and smart shoes, dressed for success, displaying ambition? Jeans and a T-shirt, showing their being casual? A tight cleavage top, a seductive choice? A pendant like a cross or a Buddha that shows spiritual values?

2. Notice Posture

When you read people's stance, ask yourself: do they keep their heads straight, confident? Or are they walking indecisively, a sign of low self-esteem? Do they swagger with a bloated face, a sign of a huge ego?

3. Watch for Physical Movements

- Bending and distance — watch where people lean. Generally, we're leaning towards things we like and away from those we don't like.

- Crossed arms and legs — this posture shows defensiveness, indignation, or self-protection. When people cross their legs, they appear to point the toes of the top leg towards the person with whom they are most at ease.

- Hiding one's hands — when people place their hands in their laps, pockets, or put them behind their backs, it means they're hiding something.

- Lip bites or cuticles — when people bite or brush their lips or pick their cuticles, they attempt to soothe themselves under pressure or in a tough situation.

4. Interpret Facial Expression

Emotions can be written on our faces. Deep frown lines suggest you worry or over-think. Crow's feet are the lines of a smile of joy. Pursed lips indicate resentment, disdain, or bitterness. A clenched jaw and a grinding of teeth are signs of tension.

The Second Technique: Listen to Your Intuition

You can tap into others outside the language and words of their body. Intuition is what your gut thinks, not what your brain says. If you want to understand someone, the most important thing is who the person is, not their outer traps. Intuition lets you see a richer picture than the obvious.

Checklist of Intuitive Cues

1. Feel the Goosebumps
Goosebumps are wonderful emotional tingles that communicate that we connect with people who move or encourage us or say something that strikes a chord. Goosebumps also occurs when you feel Deja-vu, a feeling that you've known someone before, even though you've never met before.

2. Pay attention to your insight
In conversations, you might get a warning about people coming in a flash. Pay attention to it. Otherwise, maybe you'll skip it. We prefer to go to the next thought so quickly that these important ideas are missed.

3. Watch for intuitive empathy
Often you can feel the physical signs and feelings of people in your body, which is an extreme form of empathy. So, when you observe people, you say, "Does my back hurt when it wasn't before? Am I sad or angry after an eventful meeting?"

The Third Technique: Sense Emotional Energy

Emotions are a beautiful representation of our life; the "work" we're giving away. We're recording these with intuition. Some people feel nice to be around; they're enhancing your mood and vitality. Others are draining; you naturally want to get out of here. This "subtle force" can be sensed inches or feet away from the body, even though it is invisible. It's called chi in Chinese medicine, a strength that is important to health.

Strategies to Read Emotional Energy

1. Sense People's Presence

This is the cumulative energy we release, not necessarily in line with words or actions. It's the emotional aura that surrounds us, like a rain cloud or the sun. As you've read, people notice: do they have a friendly personality that attracts you? Or do you get the willies to get you back off?

2. Watch People's Eyes

Our eyes are transmitting powerful energy. Much like the brain has an electric pulse reaching beyond the body, experiments show that the eyes are transmitting this, too. Take the time to look into people's eyes. Are they still caring? Sexy? Tranquil? Crazy? Angry? Also determine: is someone suggesting a potential for intimacy? Or do you think they're covered or hiding?

3. Notice the Feel of a Handshake, Hug, and Touch

We exchange emotional energy through physical interaction like an electrical current. Ask yourself, does your handshake or hug feel warm, relaxed, and confident? Or is it off-putting and you want to withdraw? Are the hands of people clamoring, showing fear. Or limp, indicating that they're uncompromising and timid?

4. Listen for Tone of Voice and Laugh

The tone and volume of our voice can say a lot about our emotions. Sound frequencies give rise to vibrations. Ask yourself, does their voice feel soothing? Or is it abrasive, snippy, or whiny?

HOW TO MAKE FRIEND

Meeting new people and making friends can be daunting, but with a little effort and willingness to venture outside your comfort zone, you can easily make friends. Start by going out there and searching for ways to socialize, including a local club or a volunteer group. As soon as you start meeting new people, take some time to get to know them and hang out together.

If you're trying to make new friends, you need to know what kind of friends you want to make. Broadly speaking, there are three types of friends:

- "Hi-Bye" colleagues or acquaintances. These are the ones you see at school/work because they are asked for in the background. You say hello when you see each other and say goodbye at the end of the day, but that's all about it. The relationship never lasts when the meaning is lost, i.e. when you leave school or work.

- Daily mates. Social, activity buddies you meet every now and then to catch up or hang out with. In general, you can talk about daily subjects under the light.

- True, friends of the soul (or best friends). People with whom you can speak about anything and all. You may or may not meet each day, but it doesn't matter as the depth of your relationship isn't measured by how much you meet — it's more than that. These are the people you can trust to be there for you anytime you need them, and they're going the extra mile for you.

Most of us are looking to make daily friends and, if possible, true friends of our souls. We've actually got a lot of hi-bye friends — more than we can count. The ratio of my hi-bye friends, regular friends, and real, soul friends is 60-30-10 per cent. Over the years that I've met more and more people, it's more like 75-20-5 per cent. I assume it's about the same for other people as well, with a difference of around 5-10 per cent.

No matter whether you're just trying to make regular or best friends, you can do that. You may not believe it, but I was a very quiet and secluded girl back in my primary and secondary school years. I kept this exclusive lifestyle while I was in junior college, even though I started talking more. Entry to university and later to P&G (my ex-company) made me more sociable. Today I run my blog and mentor others by 1-1 coaching and workshops where I share a lot of my life to others. When the younger me was thinking about what I would be like in the future, I would never have imagined that I would be as outward and vocal as I am today.

If you look at the people out there who seem to make friends easily, they were probably lonely at some point. They are all likely to have developed their social skills over time. For the same cause, through time and practice, you will learn to become more sociable.

Here Are Personal Tips To Get New Friends:

1. Realize your fear is in your head

The first step is to build a positive mental picture of meeting new people. Some of us see meeting new people as a terrifying occurrence. We're concerned about making a good impression, whether the other person is going to like us, how to keep the conversation going, and so on. The more we think about it, the more terrifying it becomes. This initial anxiety is turned into a mental terror that takes a life of its own and unknowingly blocks us from making new friends. In reality, shyness towards others is the product of fear. In reality, all these fears are in our minds. If you think about it, 99 per cent of people are too busy to be worried about this stuff themselves to pay attention to you. If you're worried about the impression you're making, they're worried about the impression they're going to create. Truth be told, they're just as afraid as you are. The remaining 1% are people who understand that a relationship is founded in a way that is deeper than concrete words or things said/done during a single experience. Even if there are people who judge you on the basis of what you do/say, are those people you want to be friends with? I don't think so.

2. Start small with people you know

If you haven't been socializing a lot, meeting a whole bunch of new people could seem daunting. If so, start little. Lower the difficulty of the task by beginning with your inner circle of friends, i.e. people you're more familiar with. There are some ways to do that:

- Get out to get to know each other. Have you got friends of a hi-bye kind from earlier years? Or have you lost contact with friends over time? Drop a nice text message and say hi. Ask for a meeting when they're free. See if there's a chance to reconnect.

- See if there are any cliques you can enter. The intention is not to break into a clique, but to practice being around new people. With them, current participants are likely to take the lead in discussions, so you can just take on the role of the observer and observe the interactions between other people.

- Get to meet the friends of your parents. You may join them in their outings or ask your friend to introduce you to them. If you're comfortable with your parents, there's a fair chance that you'll be comfortable with your peers, too.

- Allow invitations to leave. I've got mates that barely get out of here. When invited out, they refuse the bulk of the invitations because they prefer to stay at home.

Their social circles are therefore small. If you want to make more friends, you have to get out of your comfort zone and go out more often than not. If you sit at home, you can't make more friends in real life!

3. Get yourself out there

When you get to know more about your inner circle of friends, the next step would be to reach out to those you don't meet.

- Enter the discussion classes. Meetup.com is a really strong social networking platform. There are several interest groups, such as groups for artists, aspiring authors, vegetarians, board-game enthusiasts, cycling enthusiasts, etc. Take advantage of your passions and join those parties. Meetups are normally monthly depending on the community itself a great way to easily meet a lot of new people.

- Take part in workshops/courses. These serve as key forums for the meeting of like-minded citizens. Last year, I went to a personal development workshop and met a lot of nice people, some of whom I became good friends with.

- You're a mentor. The perfect way to kill two birds with one stone — not only can you spread kindness and love, but you also meet caring people with a purpose.

- Only go to the groups. Parties such as birthday parties, Christmas / New Year / Celebration parties, house warmers, functions/events, etc. It's probably a place where you'll make a lot of new friends, but not necessarily lasting relationships. Even a good way to meet more people.

- Come and enjoy the bars and clubs. A lot of people visit them to meet more friends, but I'm not recommending them because the friends you make here are probably more hi-bye friends than Type # 2 or Type # 3 friends. It's a good thing just to visit a few times and see how they are for yourself before you make a judgment.

- On-line groups. The internet is a perfect place to get to know new people. Some of my best friendships have begun online. Ten years ago, I met one of my best friends, K, from the IRC channel. I have at least two other good friends I've met online. Since then, we've met several times and become great friends. Even now, I have a lot of wonderful connections with people I've never met (other personal growth bloggers and readers). Just because we haven't met (yet) doesn't mean that we can't be great mates. Nowadays, online forums are one of the key locations where groups gather. Check out online forums on subjects of interest to you. Participate constructively and bring value to the debate. Soon, you're going to get to know the people there better.

4. Take the first step

When you're out there with the people around you, someone has to make the first move. If the other party doesn't start talking, take the first step to say hello. Share something about yourself, and then give the other party a chance to share something about it. Anything simple, like asking how the day is, or what they've done today / in the past week, is a great start to a conversation. If the ice is cracked, it's going to be easier to communicate.

5. Get to know the person

Friendship is between you and the other guy. Get to know that person as an individual Here are some issues that need to be considered:

- What is he/she doing?
- What are their hobbies?
- What was he/she up to recently?
- What are his/ her next priorities/goals?
- What does he or she respect the most?
- What are the ideals of his / her?
- What motivates him/her?
- What are his / her passions for life? Purposes? Is it dreams?

6. Connect with genuinely

Sometimes we are so wrapped up in our own concerns — such as what others think of us, what we should say next, what our next step is — that we miss the whole point of friendship. You should focus on presentation aspects such as how you look, what you say, and how you say things, but don't be obsessed about them. These acts do not (truly) describe friendship. What distinguishes friendship is the relationship between you and a mate.

Show fire, compassion, and appreciation for everyone you encounter. Do things because you want to, and not because you need to. Okay, take care of them as you would yourself. If you actively approach someone, you can attract people who really want to communicate. Your future true friends will be among them.

7. Be yourself

Don't change your mind to make new friends. That's the last thing you can do with it. Why am I doing that?
Say, by being loud, you make a lot of new friends. But your usual self is silent and introverted. What's going to happen then? It would be nice to get those new friends in the first place, but friendship has been built with you as an extrovert. This means either:

- You're always the loud, brassy person your new friends knew you as well. However, it's all going to be a facade. In the long run, it's going to be tiring to sustain this picture. Not just that, friendship is going to be built on a hollow face.

- You're going to move back to the introverted. However, your buddies are going to feel betrayed because this isn't the guy they've made friends with. They'll also progressively step away if the personalities don't match up.

- Yeah, just be you. That way, potential new friends are going to know you like you, and they're going to use that to determine whether they want to take the relationship a step further. I don't think there's a need to be outward and persuasive like Tony Robbins to make friends. It's all about you being here. The truest partnerships are formed with the two parties embracing each other for who they are.

PRACTICAL MINDFULNESS

1. Scan through the entire body for sensations.

You may have back pain or a headache, but what do you feel in your left shoulder right now? Your abdominals? Go through your body, whatever you want, to experience what you feel in various parts of it. Leave nothing out. Every sensation, no matter how tiny, is just as significant. Try not to move from one powerful feeling to the next. Why would any pieces merit more consideration just because they're sore? You will eventually get there (use common sense, though — don't want to overlook extreme pain that you should be treating). The goal is to be aware of it and then let that awareness pass through. They're both equally fine.

2. Concentrate on the breath.

A classic technique of breathing meditation is a simple way to ground yourself, to calm down, and to become conscious of your mind. There's still your air. Don't try to control it while you dwell on it. Look at it the way you find it. You may be counting your breaths, but you don't have to. You should focus on movement in your abdomen and lungs or in your nasal passages (and probably your beard, a very useful meditation assistant).

3. Isolate your senses.

Concentrate your focus on one sense at a time. You can start wherever you like. Try to get information. Look at the tree: see the leaves, the twigs, the buds, the base, and the roots. Listen to the train: hear the low roar, the clanking, and the high-pitched screeches. Feel your body: the tingle on your skin, the texture of your clothes (if applicable) and the pressure of your position. You are using the taste and smell, too. Try to capture as much truth as you can in any one context. Rest assured that you're never going to capture everything, it's all going to flow through your senses. That's how it goes, and that's all right.

4. Practice simultaneous sensory perception.

This fits well in the sense of the previous process. Attempt to experience as much information as you can with multiple senses at the same time. Start with two — the easiest thing is sight and sound. See and hear at the same time, be fully mindful of all senses. It's better because much of the sound comes from whatever you're looking at. Then pay attention to sounds coming from beyond your eye awareness as well. Second, widen the visual awareness and strive to see and hear as much as you can at once. Combine the less dominant senses with the more dominant ones. At the same time, try to listen and sense the physical sensations (closing your eyes will help). Try to see and taste at once, even though what you eat isn't in your visual vision. Later, incorporate more than two senses in your simultaneous concentration. Don't be discouraged if you find it daunting. It's not that easy. Importantly, be mindful of the senses that you want to concentrate on, and focus exclusively on them.

5. Observe moments of non-verbal thought.

A final tip is a quick form of clearing your mind. There is fascinating recent studies and evidence that all human conscious reasoning is occurring "after the reality." To simplify the idea, we seem to have an internal story that provides plausible justifications for what we are doing in a moment. This inner narrative gives us the idea that we are logical, consciously functioning individuals. The narrative inevitably occurs after our actions — not only in the case of almost unconscious activities such as driving a vehicle but also in the case of apparently highly rationalized decisions such as what stock to purchase. Even the decisions we would have sworn to be the product of reasonable reasoning may, in fact, be verbally rationalized after the decision. We plan our actions, but even in this case, we make small decisions (heuristics) as we prepare, and that's what our planning is all about. This is what our private narrative makes up, forming an impression of conscious thought. Whether this is up to debate, I believe that it functions to help our idea of a constant, enduring human personality.
Now if you're still with me, you don't have to adhere to such a progressive philosophy of mind to benefit from it. It actually adds weight to the renunciation of your internal story, at least momentarily, in order to fully live in the moment. There are times when you don't think about words. Observing and attempting to prolong such moments can require a great deal of focus. It could also be a beneficial workout.
All previous methods provide you with a focused base for this approach. Look at the lack of verbalization with your attention on touch, breathing, or multiple senses at once. There is no clarification in your head, no definition of what you're feeling. You don't need to feel what you're doing. Try to catch up and observe the moment. If you can, focus on it.

Mindfulness is a state of mind. As all human states, this is not a static objective, but a dynamic operation. Start anywhere. Good journeys.

BODY LANGUAGE

Body Language is a silent ensemble, as people continuously offer hints as to what they think and feel. Non-verbal messages, including body gestures, facial expressions, vocal tone and volume, and other signals, are commonly referred to as body language. Micro expressions (brief displays of emotion on the face), hand movements, and posture are all captured almost instantly in the human brain — even when a person is not consciously aware of something. For this purpose, body language can strongly influence how a person is viewed and how he or she, in turn, interprets the motivation, mood and openness of others. It's easy to mirror; starting from childhood, the newborn moves his body to the rhythm of the voice he hears.

How to Read Negative Body Language

Being aware of negative body language in others can allow you to pick up on unspoken issues or bad feelings. So, in this segment, we're going to illustrate some negative non-verbal signs that you should be searching for.

Difficult Conversations and Defensiveness

Difficult or awkward conversations are an inconvenient part of life at work. You may have had to deal with a difficult client, or you may have wanted to speak to someone about his or her poor performance. Or you could have signed a big deal.
Ideally, these issues would have been handled peacefully. But they are also complicated by feelings of nervousness, discomfort, defensiveness, or even resentment. And, while we can try to conceal them, these feelings are always articulated in the language of our body. For example, if someone shows one or more of the following behaviors, they are likely to be disengaged, disinterested or unhappy:

- The arms were crossed in front of the body.
- Minimal or stressed expression of the face.
- The body has turned away from you.

Avoiding Unengaged Audiences

If you need to deliver a presentation or function together in a group, you want the people around you to be 100% engaged.
Here are some "telling" signs that people may be bored or disinterested in what you say:
- Sitting bowed heads downcast.
- Looking at something else, or in space.
- Fidgeting, taking clothing, or fiddling with pens and tablets.
- Reading or teaching.

When you witness someone being disengaged, you're in a better position to do something about it. For example, you can re-engage her by asking her a direct question, or by encouraging her to add her own ideas.

How to Project Positive Body Language

If you use positive body language, it can add strength to the verbal messages or ideas you want to convey and help you avoid sending mixed or confusing signals.
In this segment, we're going to describe some of the simple postures you can take to project self-confidence and transparency.

Making a Confident First Impression

These tips can help you to adjust your body language so that you make a great first impression:
- Keep your stance open. Be happy, but please don't slouch! Sit down or stand up and place your hands on your knees. Avoid standing with your hands on your shoulders, as this will make you appear bigger, able to express anger or a desire to dominate.

- You are using your firm handshake. But don't get carried away with it! You don't want to make the other person unhappy or, worse, hurt. If it does, you're likely to come across as rude or violent.

- Keep eye contact nice. Try to hold the other person's eyes for a couple of seconds at a time. This is going to show her that you are genuine and committed. But, do not turn it into a staring match.

- Don't touch your ears. There is a common perception that people who touch their faces when answering questions are being deceptive. While this is not always true, it's best to avoid fiddling with your hair or touching your mouth or nose, particularly if your intention is to come across as trustworthy.

Public Speaking

Positive body language will also help you connect people, mask anxiety, and express confidence when you speak in public. Here are a few suggestions that will help you do this:

- Have a strong stance. Sit down or stand straight, with your hands on your back and your arms extended, on your side or in front of you. Don't be tempted to place your hands in your pockets or slouch, as this would make you appear disinterested.

- Keep your head up. Your head is expected to be straight and level. Leaning too far forward or backward can make you look aggressive or arrogant.

- Train and strengthen your stance. You must have practiced your presentation beforehand, so why don't you just practice your body language? Stand in a comfortable way, fairly dividing the weight. Hold one foot slightly ahead of the other – this will help you maintain your stance.

- Use hand gestures that are available. Stretch your hands apart, in front of you, your palms facing the audience slightly. This shows a willingness to connect and exchange ideas. Keep the upper arms close to the neck. Take care to prevent overexpression, or people can pay more attention to your hands than to what you say.

Interviews, Negotiations and Reflection

Body language will also help you remain calm in circumstances where emotions have the ability to run high – a negotiation, for example, or a performance evaluation. Using the following strategies to defuse stress and to show openness:

- Using a mirror. If you can, subtly represent the body language of the person you're talking to. This will make him feel more at ease, and he will develop a friendship. But don't copy every move he makes, as it can make him feel awkward, or you won't take him seriously.

- Relax the body. It may be difficult to keep emotions at bay, particularly in anxious circumstances such as an interview or evaluation. But you can maintain the impression of composure by keeping your hands still and avoiding fidgeting with your hair or rubbing your face.

- Look interested. As we mentioned above, rubbing your face or mouth may be a sign of dishonesty. But, it can also prove that you're aware. So, if you're asked a complicated question, it's okay to brush your cheek slightly or to stroke your jaw. This will show the other person that you are focusing on your response before you reply.

DARK PSYCHOLOGY

Dark Psychology is a study of the human condition as it relates to the psychological nature of people to prey on others driven by criminal and deviant impulses that lack the intent and general principles of instinctive drives and social science theory. All of humanity has the ability to victimize other human beings and living things. While many are restraining or sublimating this tendency, some act upon these impulses.

Dark Psychology attempts to explain certain emotions, feelings, beliefs and subjective processes that contribute to sexual activity that is antithetical to contemporary understandings of human activity. Dark Psychology believes that criminal, deviant and abusive conduct is objective and has a logical, goal-oriented motivation 99.99 per cent of the time. It's the remaining .01 per cent, Dark Psychology parts of Adler's Theory and Teleology. Dark Psychology postulates that there is an area within the human mind that causes certain individuals to perform atrocious actions without intent. The Dark Singularity has been invented in this theory.

Dark Psychology claims that all humanity has a reservoir of malevolent intent towards others, ranging from minimally obtrusive and transient thoughts to pure psychotic deviant actions without any coherent reasoning. It's called the Dark Spectrum. Mitigating factors that act as accelerators and attractors to approach the Dark Singularity, and where a person's heinous actions fall on the Dark Continuum, is what Dark Psychology calls the Dark Factor. The brief introductions to these definitions are shown below. Dark Psychology is a topic that the writer has been grappling with for fifteen years. It was only recently that he actually conceptualized the meaning, theory and psychology of this part of the human condition.

The more readers can imagine Dark Psychology, the better prepared they are to weed out their chances of victimization by human predators. It is necessary to have at least a limited understanding of Dark Psychology before continuing. The following six tenets are required to understand Dark Psychology fully:

- Dark Psychology is a basic feature of the human condition. This has had an impact throughout history. Every culture, community and the people who live in them retain this part of the human condition. The most compassionate people known to have this domain of evil, but never act upon it and have lower rates of violent thoughts and feelings.

- Dark Psychology is a study of the human condition as it relates to people's emotions, feelings, and perceptions of this inherent ability to prey upon others for simple, definable motives. Given that all action is purposeful, goal-oriented, and conceptualized by modus operandi, Dark Psychology puts forward the notion that the closer a person gets to the "black hole" of pure evil, the less likely he/she has a motivational purpose. While this writer believes that pure evil is never achieved, because it is infinite, Dark Psychology believes that there are those who come near.

- Dark Psychology may be ignored in its latent form because of its potential for misinterpretation as aberrant psychiatry. History is full of examples of this latent propensity to manifest itself as active, destructive actions. Modern psychiatry and psychology describe the patient as a psychopath who has no regret for his actions. Dark Psychology believes that there is a spectrum of intensity ranging from thoughts and perceptions of aggression to extreme victimization and abuse without a rational intent or motivation.

- In this scale, the intensity of the Dark Psychology is not perceived to be less or more abominable by the actions of victimization, but it maps a spectrum of inhumanity. A basic example would be a contrast between Ted Bundy and Jeffrey Dahmer. They were both extremely cruel in their acts. The difference is that Dahmer committed his atrocious murders on account of his illusory desire for companionship when Ted Bundy assassinated and sadistically inflicted pain on his victims as a result of pure psychological cruelty. Both will be higher in the Dark Spectrum, but one, Jeffrey Dahmer, can be best understood by his insane desperate need to be accepted.

- Dark Psychology believes that all individuals have a capacity for violence. This ability is inherent in all humans, and multiple internal and external influences increase the likelihood of this ability manifesting itself in unpredictable behaviors. These behaviors are aggressive in nature, and may often act without purpose. Dark Psychology suggests that the predator-prey relationship is corrupted by humans. Dark Psychology is essentially a psychological phenomenon and is not experienced by any other living being. Violence and disorder can occur in other living organisms, but humanity is the only species that has the ability to do so without intent.

- Understanding the root causes and effects of Dark Psychology will make it easier for society to identify, diagnose and potentially reduce the hazards inherent in its impact. Learning the principles of Dark Psychology has a twofold beneficial impact. First, by recognizing that we all have this capacity for evil, it helps those with this information to will the risk that it will explode. Second, understanding the tenets of Dark Psychology matches our original evolutionary objective of striving to survive.

MIND CONTROL

Many people use the "Mind Control" term for different things. In fact, this is a broad definition that has different types of definition. Mind control means taking control of the mind. The question is, who's the mind being controlled?

There are many different mind control procedures that are used in every situation. However, these methods may have been drawn from completely different sciences. So the methods used to manipulate the mind of other people are somewhat different from those used to manipulate our own mind. That's why there are a few forms of mind control.

But if someone wishes to alter and monitor the feelings of others, they need to practice hypnosis and NLP (Neurolinguistic Programming) techniques.

For example, using a known NLP technique, someone can manipulate a person's thoughts when he seems to be talking to him as normal. This approach is referred to as hidden or conversational hypnosis.

After a moment, the idea planted comes to the other person as a new hypothesis. Although they think they've been considering all by themselves, in fact, you've told them what to do. So you can influence and control their minds in this way.

Traditional hypnosis, on the other hand, requires the permission of the other party so that you may hypnotize them and plant ideas in their subconscious.

Another form of hypnosis that tends to be mind modification is stage hypnosis. This is a tactic used by showmen hypnotists to control a "volunteer" participant. There's a question over whether this really is a mind-control technique or a fake technique.

For those who refer to mind control as a way to manipulate their own mind, there are several means available. Some commonly held ones are self-hypnosis, the Silva technique, meditation, brainwave therapy, and many more.

In self-hypnosis, they attempt to cause their minds to hypnosis. This typically occurs with thorough visualizations by activating the right hemisphere and decreasing the volume of brain waves. These visualizations can be a simple symbolic way to accomplish their goals, to avoid unhealthy habits, to lose weight and more.

Self-hypnosis can be either guided or unguided. Driven means that someone listens to the hypnotherapist's pre-recorded guidance to fall into a trance and be hypnotized. The Internet is full of such items, which are intended for specific purposes. Any of the main goals of these services are to avoid smoking, lose weight, soothe, assist with sexual issues, and more.

The unguided form is more complicated and requires only the thinking of the individual to cause trance and hypnosis. Visualizations are primarily used for this purpose, and it is important for the person to remain centered on the technique.

The Silva mind control system is a related technique. In reality, Silva's method is taught at seminars and includes easy and precise exercises to calm the mind. One of them is a three-toe technique that improves memory on requests.

Meditation takes a particular approach to mind management. Whereas previous mind control techniques stimulate the right hemisphere and the imagination of the brain, the purpose of meditation is just the opposite: to avoid the development of thought. There are hundreds of meditation techniques available. One simple thing is concentration meditation, where a person tries to focus his attention on an internal (e.g. breathing) or an external (candle flame) fixed location.

With brainwave processing, mind control has a totally different definition compared to previous techniques. In brainwave training, regulation refers to modifying the frequency of brain waves to a given value. There are special frequencies associated with specific experiences, such as deep meditation or lucid dreaming. The only thing you need is a high-quality pair of headphones and a binary beat session. There are also other brainwave training technologies; binaural beats are the most common. So, there are isochronic tones, monaural sounds, and a photo-drive. The last one stimulates the brain with light and is very effective.

Basically, mind control is a special skill that you can master. You will still make a lot of use of this if you excel in mastering the techniques involved. There are three key explanations why you should master these techniques. Let's take a look at them.

1. To Gain Control Over Issues Bothering Your Mind

It would help if you learned a range of mind management strategies to deal with problems that concern your mind. In most instances, the human mind is the center of thought and motion. If you can't control what's going on in your mind, life can be boring for you. It is critical that you engage these simple strategies in order to take care of your mind and better your life in the process.

2. To Get the Desired Attention, You Need From Others

If you're going to have to win some fight with someone, you need to learn these strategies. When giving a lecture or speech, you will still get the audience to do or say what you want by using powerful mind control techniques. You're sure to get all the love you need from them when you use mind control tactics to win their hearts.

3. To Control Other People's Minds Positively

If you take time to gain mastery of your mind, you can easily manage to manipulate other people's minds at will. You have to be vigilant when you do this because your actions can also adversely affect other people's minds. It would help if you concentrated on using the methods that you learned in a constructive way. Through doing so, you will makethe lives of those around youbetter. If you need to understand the three key reasons listed above, you really need to take time to learn the basic concepts involved. You have to set aside some time every day in order to practice the techniques. To succeed in the process, you need to use the meditation and visualization method. In most situations, meditation really helps a lot when it comes to mind control. If you really want to see better results, you have to work.

Again, there is a need for you to employ the influence of positive thought and repentance in practicing mind management techniques. This is sure to help you produce positive outcomes by using methods to manipulate other people's minds.

In all, when you take time to explore what they are, you will still master these strategies. It is crucial that you use every resource at your disposal to master the techniques. You will greatly change your life and that of others if you succeed in mastering the simple mind control strategies that have already been made available.

CONCLUSION

Each culture develops its own rules on what is acceptable and what is not acceptable. It also seems like we are "hard-wired" to act in ways in order to make our communication more efficient. We're born with the basic skills to help us communicate with others. There's a lot more to communicating than just words. Efficient social skills make the most of all of our other communication skills.

A great way to tune your social skills is to go to a public place and wait around quietly while people mingle. Examine how they interact with each other in a social sense. In performing this exercise, it will appear very normal before someone shows a behavior that is socially unacceptable; they will be behaving against the norms of society.

Having good social skills gives you an advantage in society; people are drawn to people who have good social attitudes and don't feel awkward talking to you. Having good social skills is simply learning how to be polite, courteous, and recognizing what society considers to be the norm.

As human beings, we communicate with each other all the time and, in order to make these interactions the best we can, we need to improve our social skills to their full potential. You will learn to improve these skills and grow yourself personally by learning more about what Social Skills are and resources to help you live the life you've been meant to live.

www.ingramcontent.com/pod-product-compliance
Lightning Source LLC
Chambersburg PA
CBHW081417080526
44589CB00016B/2573